D0769989

"This book will change the way you read God's book. The Bible's story takes on fresh power and personal challenge. Your heart will be filled with hope as you sense God's relentless, loving pursuit."

—DOUGLAS CONNELLY, author of *Wisdom for Life's Journey*

"Indeed, I wanted to dance after reading this splendid presentation of the restorative narrative, which we know as the gospel of God's grace. The faith, 'once and for all delivered to the saints' comes alive in Bishop Frey's creative and faithful presentation of the rhythms of redemption."

—SCOTTY SMITH, senior pastor of Christ Community Church, Franklin, Tennessee

"Writing from a biblical perspective, and out of the deep wellsprings of his own faith, William Frey focuses much-needed attention on the neglected topic of eternal hope. He reminds readers in a clear and compelling way that we are all called to be part of God's master plan and to share in His creative activities. This book, I'm certain, will give people new courage, as it did me, to deal with the uncertainties and vicissitudes of this age, in the sure knowledge that God is in charge and that whatever happens in the future is ultimately secure."

—GEORGE GALLUP, chairman of The George H. Gallup International Institute

"With wisdom, wit, and deep compassion, Bill Frey invites readers to join him in God's amazing 'Dance of Hope.' Turn up the music and put on your dancing shoes. This is a reading experience you don't want to miss!"

—CLAIRE CLONINGER, songwriter, author, and speaker

"In *The Dance of Hope*, Bill Frey shows us with DVD clarity a vision of 'the way things are' in a church seen as God's safe house for creating new people. These honest, vulnerable, and clear-eyed women and men use uncommon sense and trans-human resources to love the poor and alienated—and anyone else they encounter, including enemies. When they are in residence at church, the purpose of these Gentle Giants is to cohost with God his Love-in party for all kinds of people."

    —J. KEITH MILLER, author of *The Taste of New Wine* and
      A Hunger for Healing

"In this thoughtfully written book, William Frey gives us a careful theological study of hope's purpose in the context of God's larger story. Sometimes a glimpse of something bigger than ourselves can be the greatest cure of all. *The Dance of Hope* offers us such a glimpse—and beckons us to widen our vision of both God and the world."

    —JOY SAWYER, licensed psychotherapist and author of *Dancing*
      to the Heartbeat of Redemption

"For over twenty-five years I have lived in Bill and Barbara Frey's extended family Christian community and have personally witnessed the truth of their lives. This book is true. I have lived it."

    —ANN B. DAVIS, Emmy Award–winning actress

"It is a rare learning opportunity indeed when a veteran churchman of the stature of Bishop Frey is willing to sum up a lifetime of thoughtful reflection on the Christian faith. This volume is a profound exploration of the reality of hope, but it is much more than that. It is the moving witness of one human being's understanding of the essence of the whole Christian vision."

    —JOHN R. CLAYPOOL, IV, Episcopal priest and author of
      Tracks of a Fellow Struggler

THE
DANCE *of*
HOPE

WILLIAM C. FREY

THE
DANCE of
HOPE

FINDING OURSELVES IN THE RHYTHM of GOD'S GREAT STORY

WATERBROOK
PRESS

THE DANCE OF HOPE
PUBLISHED BY WATERBROOK PRESS
2375 Telstar Drive, Suite 160
Colorado Springs, Colorado 80920
A division of Random House, Inc.

ISBN 1-57856-492-1

Excerpt from the hymn "Lord Christ when first thou cam'st to earth" by Walter Russell Bowie reprinted by permission. Excerpt from *Seasons of Your Heart: Prayers and Reflections,* copyright © 1991 by Macrina Wiederkehr reprinted by permission of HarperCollinsPublishers, Inc. Excerpt titled "The Creation," from *God's Trombones* by James Weldon Johnson, copyright © 1927 The Viking Press, Inc., renewed © 1955 by Grace Nail Johnson. Used by permission of Viking Penguin, a division of Penguin Putnam Inc.

Library of Congress Cataloging-in-Publication Data
Frey, William C.
   The dance of hope : finding ourselves in the rhythm of God's great story / William C. Frey.—1st ed.
      p. cm.
   Includes bibliographic references.
   ISBN 1-57856-492-1
   1. Man (Christian theology)—Biblical teaching. 2. Creation—Biblical teaching. 3. Bible—Criticism, interpretation, etc. I. Title.
   BS66 .74 2002
   233—dc21   2002008295

Printed in the United States of America
2003—First Edition

10 9 8 7 6 5 4 3 2 1

CONTENTS

Acknowledgments

This book would never have been born without the rigorous coaching of Kathleen Davis Niendorff, agent extraordinary. My thanks as well to the team at WaterBrook Press, especially Thomas Womack and Erin Healy, whose critical eyes kept me focused all along the way. And how could I begin to thank Barbara, wife of fifty years, light of my life, and companion in every joy and sorrow, for her perseverance (stubbornness) and amazing patience during fifteen years or so as I have struggled to bring these thoughts together? Truly I married above myself.

Deep thanks as well to fellow pilgrims Ann B. Davis and Lynn Ewing for their patience in reading draft after draft and for their helpful comments. I'm also grateful to a sturdy crew of the faithful from Christ Church, San Antonio, for listening and helping to hone this material during a Lenten series in 2001 that lasted long after Easter. And thanks, too, to the countless folk at conferences all around the country who have heard portions of this work and encouraged me to put it into book form. God is indeed gracious and generous.

I pray that the God of our Lord Jesus Christ, the all-glorious Father, may confer on you the spiritual gifts of wisdom and vision, with the knowledge of him that they bring. I pray that your inward eyes may be enlightened, so that you may know what is the hope to which he calls you, how rich and glorious is the share he offers you among his people in their inheritance, and how vast are the resources of his power open to us who have faith.

—EPHESIANS 1:17-19, REB

Hope is the ability to hear the melody of the future. Faith is the courage to dance to it today.

—ATTRIBUTION UNKNOWN

THE POWER OF HOPE

If, as C. S. Lewis said, "joy is the serious business of heaven," then hope must be the serious business of the church. One of the greatest gifts Christians can offer the world is a fresh infusion of hope. Our society's supply is running very low.

Not that there aren't lots of people out there offering hope. Madison Avenue does it twenty-four hours a day, blatantly trumpeting the "fact" that your life will be infinitely better if you buy their cola, their car, their cosmetics. But experienced people have learned to mute their televisions during the commercials.

And then there are the politicians. I write this during an election year and every day am made more aware of the fact that politicians understand the intoxicating power of hope better than most others. They depend on it to score big in every election. "The future will be better," they say, "with me in office." "We can solve all the problems caused by our opponents." "Prosperity is just around the corner." So great is the need for hope in the human psyche that we fall for it over and over again. "This time it will be different," we say to ourselves. But deep inside we know better. We've had our fingers burned too often.

In a sort of caricature of the American dream, too many of us have come to believe that we're automatically entitled to "the good things in life"—a good job with great benefits and a generous retirement plan, constant upward mobility, the perfect family, wonderful children, unfailing health, the latest gadgets, and season tickets to whatever it is we most enjoy. When any of these things fail to materialize (and they invariably do), we complain that our dreams have been shattered. In fact, if anything has been shattered it's our illusions. And the shattering of illusions usually results in cynicism and despair.

Few people would deny that we live in a society that is increasingly prone to despair, one in which Prozac is becoming as common as peppermint. According to a major psychology magazine, clinical studies have revealed a tenfold increase in clinical depression among people in the United States during the last two generations. A gift of hope would be an enormous blessing.

But it would have to be the real thing, not some cheap substitute like optimism, which is usually based on some naive view of human nature with an added dose of wishful thinking. It would have to be based on fact, not fiction. And the offer would have to come from people whose lives it has visibly transformed.

Hope is what keeps us alive. It's a stimulant that is much more powerful than any mind-altering drug and whose effects are not limited to the mind or the spirit. Our immune system responds both to the presence and the absence of hope. Hopeful people are healthier people. Hopeless people are susceptible not only to depression but to disease as well.

True hope has the power to diminish the effects of adversity. We've all met people who, on the surface, seem to have little to live for, but whose lives nonetheless are sparkling examples of joy, vitality, and hope. Phillips Brooks, a nineteenth-century bishop in Massachusetts who wrote "O Little Town of Bethlehem," was once asked what he considered the greatest proof of the truth of Christianity. He replied, "An aunt of mine who lives in New Hampshire."

We all know people whose personal circumstances, we imagine, would crush us if we were to suffer the same fate, and yet they give evidence of a remarkable inner peace and strength. Some of them triumph over material poverty, others over physical or emotional disabilities, and still others over unspeakable personal tragedies. But they all have one thing in common. They hope. And contrary to our current popular value system, their hope is not a purely materialistic one. It isn't a matter of the poor hoping that someday they'll buy a winning lottery ticket, or of the paralyzed dreaming that they will walk again. It's hope of a different nature that keeps them so strongly alive.

Their testimony says, "No circumstances, internal or external, personal or environmental, will be permitted to define who and what I am, nor will they have the last word about what I may become." Their identity is not the product of their immediate circumstances. It comes from somewhere else.

Sometimes it sounds like an almost defiant challenge, the sort of thing Job said while he was wrestling with his less-than-helpful friends: "I know that my Redeemer lives, and that at the last he will stand upon the earth; and after my skin has been thus destroyed, then in my flesh I shall see God, whom I shall see on my side, and my eyes shall behold, and not another" (Job 19:25-27). And sometimes it's simply a peaceful surrender to the will and purposes of a loving God, as in Jesus' words from the Cross, "Father, into your hands I commend my spirit" (Luke 23:46). Whatever the form, hope carries with it a triumphant vitality.

And what of those without hope? In *The Inferno,* Dante tells us that the sign above the gates of hell says, "Abandon hope, all ye who enter here." And Eric Fromm says that the "person who has given up hope...has entered the gates of hell, whether he knows it or not, and has left behind him his own humanity."

Hope is the conviction that things—the things that, in the final analysis, matter the most—will someday be better. It's "the melody of the future." Or as one modern theologian put it, hope means that "whatever happens, the future is secure."

How desperately we need that gift!

The Erosion of Hope

But who can give such a gift, and on what can it be based? The logical source should be the Christian community. After all, the Christian gospel provides the only solid foundation for lives grounded in hope. But sadly, even there hope is often in short supply.

Though it's mentioned in the Bible almost two hundred times (and many more, if you include the hundreds of "fear nots"), hope has become the Cinderella of Paul's famous trinity of "faith, hope, and love." Thousands of books have been written about faith and love, but far fewer speak to us about hope. A widely used study guide lists a dozen major biblical themes, and while faith and love are near the top, hope isn't mentioned at all.

When we examine our deficits as Christians, a loss of hope may not be the first thing that springs to mind. Its disappearance is usually imperceptible, the result of a long, slow process of erosion that washes away the fertile topsoil of our faith, leaving the barren rock exposed. And after a while we begin to believe that this barrenness is the natural condition of Christians and that spiritual aridity is somehow normal, even virtuous.

Many of us would confess to living with a sort of spiritual malaise, perhaps even some degree of depression. This malaise may begin with the subtle suspicion that something is missing in our Christian life. Almost unconsciously we feel that the practice of our Christian faith ought to be yielding greater results than it does. We go through the motions of worship, Bible study, and prayer without experiencing anything like the "glorious inheritance" and "vast resources of power" that Paul speaks about in the passage quoted at the beginning of this introduction. There seems to be a huge chasm between Paul's expectations and our own experience. While we may not know exactly what Jesus had in mind when he promised us "life in abundance," we suspect that we haven't yet found it. And if we identify with any biblical character, it's probably a doubting Thomas, or the anonymous man who said to Jesus, "I believe; help my unbelief!" (Mark 9:24).

If someone were to ask us, we would say that we have deep admiration for the truly joyful and hopeful Christians we meet. But secretly we assume that they must be among the fortunate few who have never had any real problems or that they're in denial about something or that their faith is superficial. After all, that's more tolerable than admitting they've discovered something we have overlooked or, for some reason, have been denied.

When we pray we often feel that our words simply bounce off the ceiling. We sometimes suspect that the line is busy, and on our bad days we even begin to doubt that there *is* a line. We wonder why our lives lack the transforming power of Christ that we read about in the Bible and that we occasionally see in other people. Why does our faith seem so weak, or even irrelevant, as we struggle with our daily difficulties—the conflicts within our families, our concerns about our jobs and job security, our anxieties about our health, our apprehensions about growing old, or our own personal pain or that of our loved ones? How do we make the connections between all of these problems and what we profess to believe?

And so we keep plodding along, hoping that God will come out of hiding, as we search for some tangible sign that the Holy Spirit is at work in our lives. And we ask ourselves, in the words of the old song, "Is that all there is?" Why, we say, though we count ourselves as conscious and intentional Christians, do we so frequently feel like those people Jesus described as "harassed and helpless, like sheep without a shepherd"? In short, we seem to fit John Wesley's description of Christians who "have just enough religion to make them miserable." Why do *we* need a fresh infusion of hope just like everybody else?

A Question of Story

I'm convinced that one of the major reasons for our lack of hope, for our spiritual malaise, is that we've forgotten who we are. We've lost our memory and suffer from a sort of spiritual Alzheimer's. And having lost our memory, we've lost our identity.

In late 1997 at the War Crimes Tribunal in The Hague, a witness, testifying in the matter of genocide in Rwanda, told an astounding story. He told of a pregnant Tutsi woman who, just before she was raped and killed by a Hutu invader, handed her tormentor a book and said, "Take this Bible, for it is our memory, and because you do not know what you are doing."

This anonymous woman's testimony reflects a deeply powerful Christian spirituality, one literally capable of enabling her to love her immediate—and homicidal—enemy. But it also bears witness to an amazing comprehension of the Bible, of the Bible's place and purpose in the lives of ordinary Christians, and of the power of the biblical story to transform and transfigure human personality and experience. The Bible is indeed our memory, and when we lose it, for whatever reason, we don't know what we're doing.

A prominent theologian, reflecting on the current intellectual and moral fragmentation in Western society, said: "It is all a question of story. We are in trouble just now because we don't have a good story. We are in between stories. The Old Story—the account of how the world came to be and how we fit into it—is not functioning properly, and we haven't learned the New Story. The Old Story sustained us for a long period of time. It shaped our emotional attitudes, provided us with life purpose, guided education. We awoke in the morning and knew where we were…everything was taken care of because the story was there…it provided a context in which life could function in a meaningful manner."[1]

The "Old Story" is, of course, the Bible. And if the story isn't functioning properly, one of the main reasons is that it's been forgotten, or it was poorly learned in the first place. My thesis is that we don't so much need to learn a new story as to recapture the old one.

But we need to recapture it in a fresh way that reveals the wonder and excitement inherent in the story itself. We need to let it speak not simply to our minds, so that we might give mental assent to Christian propositions about truth, nor to our hearts alone, so that we might form a sentimental attachment to the things of God, but to our imaginations, so that our hearts, minds, and wills will be stirred to active participation in the mighty acts that God is still doing in our own day and time.

Jesus once made a pointed reference to biblical blindness and to the need for a cure. The occasion was one of those stump-the-Rabbi days when Jesus' enemies, like a mob of hungry reporters hounding a politician, tried to trick him into saying something incriminating. After successfully fending off the Pharisees with his render-to-Caesar remark, he was approached by a group of Sadducees. These were the urbane, sophisticated, powerful, and well-connected folk who, unlike the orthodox Pharisees, denied the resurrection of the dead, claiming it wasn't taught in the Torah, the Jewish Law.

They told him a hoary old rabbinical story about a woman who had married into a family that, apparently, suffered from some grave genetic defect. She married the first of seven brothers, but he died without having fathered a child. She then married the second brother and the same thing happened, and so on through all seven. Finally, the woman herself died.

The Sadducees then popped their how-to-embarrass-a-fundamentalist question: "Rabbi, in this (ahem) *resurrection,* whose wife will she be, since she had married all seven?"

Jesus refused to dignify the query with a direct answer but simply told them that they were totally clueless ("ye therefore do greatly err") because they knew "neither the Scriptures nor the power of God." He then proceeded to show them, from one of their own favorite texts, just how wrong they were.[2]

One of the things to remember about this brief encounter is that the Sadducees were not biblical illiterates. In fact, they had some characteristics in common with modern-day fundamentalists. They knew the words, but they hadn't heard the music. They had *read* the Scriptures, but Jesus said they didn't *know* the Scriptures. In other words, they were familiar with the text as religious information, but they had not yet learned to view the text as an invitation to an experiential encounter with the living God. His challenge to them was to take a fresh look at familiar words and to find in them the power of God to offer new life, even to the dead.

Memory Loss

The loss of our biblical memory can be traced to a number of causes. The first and most obvious one is that few people invest the time and effort necessary to master the Book. A survey by *Christianity Today* revealed that even those evangelical Christians whose boast is in the Bible share in American society's biblical illiteracy to an alarming degree.

Even when we do try to know the Scriptures, we find it hard to connect the dots and see the whole biblical picture. Many of us shy away from the Bible because we have too much trouble sorting out the plot. There doesn't seem to be any recognizable thread running through it that we can take hold of. A modern author says, "Though the Bible is full of literature's two great themes, love and death (as well as its exciting caricatures, sex and violence), it's also full of tedious ritual prescriptions and interminable battles."[3] And besides, so many of the names are strange and unfamiliar. We can handle Abraham, Isaac, and Jacob, but what about Abel-Beth-Maachah or Maher-Shalal-Hash-Baz?

Another reason we have lost our biblical memory is that most people fail to see the connection between the Old Testament and the New and therefore misunderstand, or understand only fragmentarily, a great deal of what they do read. Even among those who do read the Bible, the Old Testament generally gets short shrift. Someone recently complained that among Christians the New Testament is required reading whereas the Old Testament is thought of as elective. At least one of the reasons for this is that old misconception about the supposed conflict between the so-called God of wrath and vengeance of the Old Testament and the God of love and mercy of the New.

An influential and controversial second-century teacher, Marcion, actually posited the existence of two different Gods. Christians must reject the Old Testament and its God of law and justice, he said, in favor of an abbreviated New Testament whose God, the Father of Jesus, is a God of love and salvation. Though Marcionism was eventually branded as heresy, it would not be too much of an exaggeration to say that Marcion may have lost the battle, but he won the war. While we may no longer believe in two Gods, some seem to think that, during the years between the Testaments, God must have gone into therapy.

By way of contrast, I once heard a prominent biblical theologian claim, with a bit of hyperbole that scholars occasionally use, that the only really important part of the Bible is the Old Testament. The New, he said, was simply a brief appendix added to let people know that the Old Testament promises had all come true!

But there's more. Even when we know the biblical story, there's still the question of whether we understand the story. Many of us fail to see how it's connected to our day-to-day lives and experiences, how its worldview is to be understood in the light of the presuppositions of modern society. Some of us are almost schizophrenic, trying to live with one view of reality that we exercise in "religious" settings and a totally different understanding of reality that we use the rest of the time.

We might believe, for example, that Jesus and some of his followers healed the sick with a touch, but we have difficulty believing that such things could happen today in what we call the "real world." We might even accept the fact that Jesus was raised from the dead but fail to see the relevance of that event to the common things of everyday life—the way we earn our money and the way we spend it, how we make and maintain our relationships with other people, the way we behave in a traffic jam or in a checkout line, how we educate our children and pass on to them the values we treasure.

And finally, if we've been unable to make the necessary connections between the biblical story and our own, it may well be because of the lenses we've been using to read it. For centuries we've been unconsciously selective in the way we interpret the biblical story. We've done it primarily through what may be called a "salvation lens." "What must I do to be saved?" has been the major question of the Western church. That's an important question, to be sure, but it isn't the only one that needs to be asked. Thomas Berry traces this selectivity back to the fourteenth century, to the impact of the Black Death, which devastated the Western—and Christian—world. Whatever theological optimism there may have been about this present life was shattered when the plague swept across Europe. How would the church respond to the annihilation of such a large number of its members? By concentrating almost exclusively on the life of the world to come.

"Within traditional Christianity there was an intensification of the faith experience," said Berry, "an effort to activate supernatural forces with special powers of intervention…the redemption mystique became the dominant form of Christian experience." He blamed this "excessive emphasis on redemption" for the neglect of the doctrine of Creation, which had been one of the primary concerns of Christian thinkers during the church's early centuries.[4]

In Western Christianity, then, our primary lens has been the one that highlights those parts of the story described in the second paragraph of the Christian creed that speaks of Jesus' life, death, and resurrection on our behalf, "who for us and for our salvation came down from heaven." We've become so comfortable looking at our biblical picture through this salvation lens that we've forgotten there are other lenses, and more often than not, we're unaware of what we're doing.

When, in recent years, we've begun to use a secondary lens, it has come from the third paragraph of the creed that speaks of the role of the Holy Spirit in the church and in the lives of believers. We might call this the "pneumatic lens," which comes from *pneuma,* the Greek word for "spirit." Since the Pentecostal revival of the early 1900s and the charismatic movement that began in the 1960s, there has been a renewed awareness of the active role of the Holy Spirit in the church and the world.

However, there's yet another lens, and until we use it, our picture of the biblical story will still be incomplete. It's the "Creation lens," the one that comes from the first paragraph of the creed that describes the creative activity of God the Father, "maker of heaven and earth, of all that is, seen and unseen." It isn't a question of our having had a mistaken understanding of the Christian faith in the past; it's more a question of incompleteness. While the salvation and pneumatic lenses do give us a recognizable and useable image, they don't give us the whole picture. Without the Creation lens, our picture, like a television with the color filters out of balance, will lack the full intensity and beauty of the original. Our memory will be deficient, and our identity incomplete.

Come along on a journey that will enable us to recover the missing parts of our story, a journey that will reveal the fullness of our identity in Christ, the glorious hope that was present in God's original plan for the world. Come and see the Christian community as the bearer of God's hope for the whole cosmos. Come and learn to hear "the melody of the future" and discover how to dance to that melody today.

In the beginning God created...
—GENESIS 1:1, KJV

In the beginning was the Word...
—JOHN 1:1

*The first man, Adam, became a living being; the last Adam became
a life-giving spirit.... Just as we have borne the image of the man
of dust, we will also bear the image of the man of heaven.*
—1 CORINTHIANS 15:45,49

United to Christ—New Creation!
—2 CORINTHIANS 5:17,
AUTHOR'S TRANSLATION
FROM THE GREEK

ONE

WHERE WE CAME FROM

The Context

In order to use a Creation lens, we'll have to examine the creation itself. The concept of a new creation, which we'll explore in much greater detail, doesn't mean a great deal unless we understand something about the first one. And this cannot be done by simple prooftexting. After all, a text without the context easily becomes a pretext. We need to understand how the individual pieces fit into the whole story. And that brings us back to our original problem. Knowing the story—the whole story.

What we need to find is a simple narrative thread that binds it all together, a sort of mental clothesline on which we can hang all the pieces. Scholars call such a clothesline a "metanarrative"—a story within a story. Perhaps the most frequently used metanarrative is "Creation, Fall, and Redemption." I once heard someone abbreviate it even more when, with a nod to John Milton, he said the story is about "Paradise Lost" and "Paradise Regained." In 1998 the renowned biblical scholar Bruce Metzger gave a masterful address in which he outlined the story under five headings:

1. Old Testament—Preparation
2. Gospels—Manifestation
3. Acts—Propagation
4. Epistles—Explanation
5. Revelation—Consummation

In the years immediately preceding the ministry of Jesus, the famous Rabbi Hillel said that a wise scholar should be able to recite the Law and the Prophets while standing on one leg. He, too, was seeking a metanarrative, a simple outline for teaching a lot of complex material. You'll recall that Jesus was once asked what is the "greatest commandment," and I always picture him, with a nod to Hillel, standing on one leg as he replied, "Love the Lord your God with all your heart, soul, mind, and strength, and your neighbor as yourself" (Mark 12:30-31, author's paraphrase).

Let me offer my own metanarrative that helps me keep the story in focus. As with all such attempts, it risks trivializing an amazingly profound and complex subject, something like reducing astronomy (with all of its distant galaxies, spiral nebulae, red dwarfs, black holes, quasars, and cosmic strings) to "Twinkle, Twinkle, Little Star," and it undeniably leaves a number of blank spaces. Nonetheless, it may be helpful to some.

The story begins with a description of Creation, a sort of dream in God's mind that takes on physical reality as God speaks a creative word. It's a dream of goodness and beauty, a universe in which all things work together in harmony and peace, the kind of universe we fantasize about when things aren't going too well. Then comes an episode describing a rebellion against God's design and the terrible consequences that flow from the spoiling of the dream. All of this takes place in the opening chapters of Genesis.

The rest of the story is filled with descriptions of all the attempts that have been made to undo the results of the rebellion and to put back together those things that have been torn apart. None of the proposed remedies seem to work adequately, but there are prophetic promises of something better, promises that aren't answered within the framework of the Old Testament itself, leaving it to close on a note of "to be continued."

The New Testament is the story of how these promises have begun to be fulfilled through God's conclusive intervention in human affairs through the life, death, and resurrection of Jesus, reversing the downward spiral of rebellion, fragmentation, and despair. It's the story of the inauguration of the true new age in which those who respond to God's action in Christ may begin to experience something of the goodness of God's original dream even as they eagerly wait for its final consummation.

In outline form the story looks something like this:

1. Creation—God's dream
2. Fragmentation—human resistance
3. Experimentation—Ark, Law, and Sword
4. Future Prophesied—promised transformations
5. New Creation—promises fulfilled, new age inaugurated
6. Heavenly Consummation

God's Dream

The quest for understanding the origin and development of the universe has fascinated me since I was a child. Growing up in the South, I can still remember schoolyard debates about the Bible and evolution, engaged in by teenagers who knew little about either one. I later learned that the firmness with which an opinion is held is generally in inverse proportion to the amount of knowledge on which it is based.

If I hadn't been led to study theology, I might well have pursued a career in physics or cosmology. Interestingly enough, there's at least one point of convergence between the Genesis story and the results of much contemporary cosmological thinking.

Among scientists, the big bang theory is currently favored. I like the idea, and it certainly works well with the biblical picture of Creation. But I find it somewhat ironic that scientists coined such a phrase in the first place.

Shouldn't they be the first to remind us that in the first moment of time, when that primordial and tightly compacted mass of hydrogen molecules exploded, there was no atmosphere to conduct sound? Had there been an observer somehow standing outside the rapidly expanding universe, he or she would not have heard anything. However, the observer would have *seen* something—no big bang, but a spectacular big light. The explosion, the collision of billions of particles of matter and antimatter, would have produced fireworks beyond the capacity of our imagination to picture.

In view of the fact that the first recorded words of God are "Let there be light" (Genesis 1:3), a scientist recently commented on the "strange coincidence" that a document thousands of years old "should have placed electromagnetic radiation at the first moment of Creation." You don't have to take Genesis as an account of the universe's first few billion years in order to admit that it got the beginning right.

This is not, by the way, the beginning of a defense of Genesis as science. Since my metanarrative offers a brief trip through the Bible, there's no need to take along the excess baggage of the battles, past and present, between fundamentalism, literalism, creationism, evolutionism, and whatever other "isms" there may be. I simply want to concentrate on what the story itself *says*.

The story of Creation, though brief, is very profound. And while the major thrust of this present writing has to do with the new creation, it helps greatly to remind ourselves of some of the characteristics of the first one. Only when we understand what was lost will we be able to appreciate how it might be recovered.

Scholars like to remind us that there are really two separate stories. The first begins with Genesis 1:1 and concludes with 2:3; the second begins with Genesis 2:4 and concludes with 4:23. For our purposes here, the debate over whether it's two stories glued together or one story told from two distinct viewpoints is immaterial. We want to look at what the story says, not where it came from. However, I want to point out that the combination of the two parts is ingenious and essential to a full understanding of human nature.

The first part tells us of original goodness. God looked at what he had made and pronounced it good. The second part brings in a needed corrective as it describes our all-too-human ability to spoil that original goodness through what we call original sin. Exclusive emphasis on the former can lead us to a totally unwarranted optimism about human nature and to the assertion that whatever is, is good. The latter, in isolation, might give us a picture of "total depravity" far beyond anything John Calvin had in mind.

The most obvious point the story makes is found in its opening line, "In the beginning, God created the heavens and the earth." The universe is not the result of some random or accidental process, but rather it has been brought forth from the mind of God with a purpose. The spiritual and psychological implications of such a simple statement are hard to overestimate. We're here because of a plan or a dream of God. And perhaps the most audacious assertion, one that sets this Jewish understanding of origins apart from all others, is that what we call history is linear rather than cyclical. It's going someplace. Life is not simply, as one southern writer put it, "an unruly swarm of random events." It has both purpose and direction. The belief that there *is* a plan, even when we don't have a clue just what it might be, has been a sturdy spiritual lifeboat for countless millions over the centuries.

As a sort of running commentary on the first sentence, the story moves to the specifics of what was done on each of the biblical "days," described in Jewish fashion as beginning with the evening—"And there was evening and there was morning, one day." With just a bit of our own creative imagination, we can imagine God, each day, stepping back and looking at what he had made and, without a hint of false modesty, saying, "That's good!" And why shouldn't it be? It's all the work of One who, by definition, does only good things. The universe has God's fingerprints all over it—though distinct from its Creator, it partakes of God's own nature.

Human beings come last, made "in the image and likeness" of God, or perhaps "*as* the image and likeness of God." Neither the man nor the woman can reflect the fullness of God's image alone. They stand side by side as peers, and their union is the union of opposites. They need each other for wholeness, and together they are given—the order is important— first a blessing, then instructions for maintaining the created order.

The numbering of the days and the progression of the things created reveal that within every constituent part, there's an order and a pattern. The universe is the product of painstaking design. We are, indeed, "fearfully and wonderfully made" (Psalm 139:14). And in a telling aside, the story speaks of leisure and rest after all the creative activity. Seemingly, God's power is not exhausted, and after the finishing touches are put on the creation, God sets the example for all of us and invents the Sabbath rest.

The second part of the Creation story has a somewhat different flavor, more like a narrative than a catalog. One of its most winsome aspects is the way in which God is painted in such clearly human terms. The Bible is wonderfully anthropomorphic!

I'm impatient with those who view anthropomorphism as a sort of mindless primitivism that sophisticated people should have outgrown long ago. Metaphors are metaphors, after all, and one with personality is prob- ably closer to the mark than some of the philosophical abstractions of the theologians, such as the "ground of all being," or the "prime mover." A British theologian remarked, "Anthropomorphism is the highest compli- ment that humanity can pay to Divinity." So long as we recognize the vast gulf that separates *any* of our images of God from the reality the image is intended to represent, we might well encourage the use of anthropomorphism. The Christian gospel, after all, is founded on the fact that God ministered to our needs in this department by taking on human flesh in Jesus.

Few people have captured the spirit of this story as beautifully as the great African American poet James Weldon Johnson in his book of poems, *God's Trombones:*

Then God walked around,
And God looked around
On all that He had made.
He looked at His sun,
And He looked at His moon,
And He looked at His little stars;
He looked on His world
With all its living things,
And God said: "I'm lonely still."

Then God sat down—
On the side of a hill where He could think;
By a deep, wide river He sat down;
With His head in His hands,
God thought and thought,
Till He thought: "I'll make me a man!"

Up from the bed of the river
God scooped the clay;
And by the bank of the river
He kneeled Him down...
Like a mammy bending over her baby,

Kneeled down in the dust
Toiling over a lump of clay
Till He shaped it in His own image;

Then into it He blew the breath of life,
And man became a living soul.
Amen. Amen.[1]

We learn that "in the cool of the day" this anthropomorphic God walks in this lush and productive garden he has planted. On one of his sojourns, he appears to examine his "mud man" and to sense Adam's loneliness. "It is not good for the man to be alone," he says. It's almost as though God said, "Oops! There seems to be something missing." Adam needs a "help meet" (Genesis 2:18, KJV).

Now, we've all taken Biology 101 or its equivalent, and we know what it is that Adam needs. So long as the man remains alone, there will be no offspring, no continuation of his species. In this part of the story, God doesn't seem to have figured this out yet. So from the same raw material from which the man was made, God creates animals and brings them to Adam to see if somehow they can serve as helpmeets for the man. As high priest of creation, Adam has the privilege of naming his fellow creatures, and so he does. But I don't think his heart was in it. The longing for companionship was too deep for any animal to satisfy.

Adam is obviously disappointed, so Plan B is put into operation. God puts Adam into a deep sleep, opens his side, extracts a rib, closes his side, does something with the rib to turn it into Eve, brings her to Adam, wakes him up, and presumably says, "What do you think about this?!" The text tells us that he replied, "This at last is bone of my bones and flesh of my flesh," but he may have also said, "Aha! Now you're talking!"

⌣

The picture of the Garden of Eden is idyllic. It's a world without "danger, sorrow, or any kind of trouble."[2] As peers, the man and the woman stand side by side in unity and harmony. There is peace between them and the rest of the created order. The garden provides for them from its abundance, and God walks and speaks with them face to face. In them, the universe has been brought to consciousness, and as priests of the natural order, they offer sacrifices of praise and thanksgiving. It's the sort of world we've come to expect from a Disney production. It is Aslan's country. It's a working definition of the Hebrew word *shalom*. It is the "Peaceable Kingdom." In short, it is paradise.

Adam and Eve are given "dominion" over the rest of creation. They're the stewards of God's handiwork, caretakers in the sense that they're called to exercise the same care and love for the world that God exhibited in bringing it into being. From the very beginning human beings are called to share in the creative activity of God. Something in our very nature leads us to bring order out of chaos. Admittedly, our creativity is derivative—we do not create *ex nihilo,* "out of nothing"—but we'll search out the infinite possibilities already present in the universe through God's primordial creative action. We'll mix and match the potentialities of the universe, find the symphonies hidden within the scales, create a community from the people around us, unlock the secrets of the material order to power a city or invent a vaccine. Children of a Creator are creative.

Then suddenly, all the peace, the beauty, the order, and the harmony of God's dream are shattered.

"You Will Be Like God"

An old *New Yorker* cartoon shows a crater-strewn landscape on a small planet where a spaceship from Earth has just landed. In the lower left-hand corner, at some distance from the spaceship, a Garden-of-Eden scene is being played out. Beneath a strange-looking tree with a serpent coiled around it, an extraterrestrial Adam is watching as an antennaed Eve reaches for the forbidden fruit. An astronaut is racing toward the scene shouting, "Miss! Oh, Miss! For God's sake, STOP!"

What would the world look like without our human tendency to spoil it? We'll never know. The existence of evil in our world is undeniable. Our capacity to hurt and destroy, to twist, distort, and disfigure the finest gifts that God gives us is universal, or as one of my friends is fond of quoting, "Human nature is evenly distributed." I need search no further than the darkest corners of my own personality to discover it, and it's cold comfort indeed to realize that I'm not alone in my predicament.

This simple fact of evil, however, seems to pose a number of questions for every thinking person. One of the questions asks, "Where does it come from?" After the passing of one of history's bloodiest centuries, when we ask why apparently normal people do horrible things to one another, we receive an almost endless list of responses, many of them mutually contradictory. Is the source of our pain heredity or environment? Is it low self-esteem or the result of thinking too much of ourselves? Is it the abuses we've suffered at the hands of others? Is it an inequitable political and social system that rewards the powerful and punishes the weak? Is it lack of freedom or lack of equality? Can it be chalked up to some sort of mental or psychological maladjustment? Is it the fault of others or our own responsibility? And the list goes on.

Another question is perhaps a little less obvious: "Why are we surprised?" We assume that the present state of affairs, the only one we've ever been familiar with, is somehow strange and abnormal. That in itself is a curious fact. After all, this is the way the world has always been since the dawn of recorded history. None of us has ever lived in an idyllic Eden.

While many of us occasionally get nostalgic for "the good old days," in our more rational moments we know that they weren't really all that good and that history has no record of a time when all people lived in peace with their neighbors. When we're confronted with the reality of human evil, whether in a European Holocaust, a genocidal conflict in Rwanda, a school-yard shooting, the unmasking of greed and corruption in local politics, or a case of domestic violence, what is it that makes us say, almost instinctively, "It's not supposed to be this way!"?

Obviously, a victim of violence or inequity has a right to complain. But the very fact that evil exists, even when it doesn't affect us directly, even when it doesn't intrude into our own personal comfort zone, nonetheless makes us uncomfortable. I believe it was C. S. Lewis who, in reflecting on this question, pointed out that fish don't feel wet in water, whereas we do. Water is not our natural environment. In similar fashion, the biblical stories of Creation make it clear that our current condition is not our natural environment either. We were created with something better in mind. Our truce with the status quo is an uneasy one, and we're uneasy about it. It's almost as if we have a kind of unconscious memory, some bit of data stuffed away in our DNA that constantly reminds us of better times—a nostalgia for better times in the past and a desperate hope for better times in the future.

J. R. R. Tolkien put it this way: "But certainly there was an Eden on this very unhappy Earth. We all long for it, and we are constantly glimpsing it: our whole nature at its best and least corrupted, its gentlest and most humane, is still soaked with the sense of 'exile'."[3] We are outside Eden, and as if that weren't enough, there's a residual memory of having been inside—and a "memory" of that future time when God's dream will be fulfilled. Frederick Buechner imagines Eve in her exile yearning for that time "when *too good not to be true* hadn't yet turned into *too good to be true;* when being alone was never the same as being lonely."[4]

How did we lose our original blessing? What was it that soured God's dream of a beautiful and harmonious world? The story gives us a disarmingly simple answer that cuts to the heart of the matter. It was not—as some shallow critics occasionally assert—sex, and it certainly wasn't an apple.

The Serpent seems to have discovered the one apparent weakness in God's armor, one limit to God's power, one seeming flaw in the design, and he immediately sets out to exploit it. He knows that the one thing the omnipotent God most desires—the free and loving response of the human heart—is something that cannot be secured by an exercise of power. The moment such an offering is compelled, it ceases to be itself. Although true love always binds us to the beloved, the act of giving that love in the first place must be free. The beauty of the original dream depends not only on the imagination and skill of the dreamer but also on the receptiveness, the loving collaboration of those who have been the products of the dream. And so the Serpent moves to undermine the trusting relationship between creatures and Creator.

The seduction to eat the forbidden fruit on the "tree of the knowledge of good and evil" is a temptation to deny our origins and our true nature and to pretend that we can be autonomous and self-sufficient. "You will be like God, knowing good and evil," the Serpent says, implying that God is holding out on us, that God hasn't given us sufficient wisdom for ordering our common lives, that we need to add something to our store of knowledge, that we ourselves need to be the ultimate arbiters of good and evil. Someone once said that the Fall was the temptation to add to the knowledge of good the knowledge of evil. Paul refers to it as the attempt to "snatch at equality with God" (Philippians 2:6, NEB).

A number of years ago when I served as president of an Episcopal seminary, I designed an ad to be placed in a Christian magazine, touting the advantages of studying in our institution. The centerpiece was the classical

Albrecht Dürer engraving of the temptation, picturing Adam and Eve, their modesty protected only by a couple of fig leaves, and the Serpent coiled around the tree with the forbidden fruit in its mouth. The lead text (in what I thought was a particularly clever double entendre) said, "Wisdom doesn't grow on trees."

The Fall wasn't simply a matter of pride, says the story. Adam and Eve were not being persuaded to think too highly of themselves. After all, it would be hard for people who were made in the image and likeness of God, who were loved personally and unconditionally by the God of Creation, and who were given the awesome responsibility of caring for the earth, to have too lofty an opinion of themselves. What more could you be? Rather, they were being seduced into thinking *wrongly* of themselves. They were talked into idolatry, into abandoning their worship of the one true God. It wasn't that they decided to make their own decisions—that's a part of being human—they were talked into making the *wrong* decision, into placing themselves at the center of their own universe.

Such idolatry is its own punishment, says William Willimon, the chaplain at Duke University. "It is painful not to be who we were created to be. We were created to worship the true and living God whom we have met in Jesus the Christ... Our hearts are restless until they find rest in the God whom we were created to worship."[5]

East of Eden

While a number of modern commentators describe all of this as a parable of maturity, as a story of humanity's "fall upward" into greater responsibility, the story itself calls it a flight into irresponsibility. The story as told is not without some almost comic overtones. Adam and Eve are apparently aware of the fact that their brief flirtation with autonomy and independence has backfired. They're ashamed and they try to hide from God, but it is God's garden after all, and they are found out and confronted.

Adam's defense is so prototypical of our own when we're caught in our misdeeds that it's easy to see why we're called Adam's offspring. The fruit doesn't fall far from the tree. Adam tries to shift the blame to Eve, and in such a way that the fault seems to be God's: "The woman *you gave me* tempted me." This is, of course, an inadvertent admission of personal guilt. A *Frank and Ernest* comic strip pictured a happy Adam greeting a perplexed Eve with, "I'm sure glad you showed up! There wasn't anybody around to blame everything on."

But life is not a comic strip, and whatever else the story may tell us, one thing is abundantly clear. Actions have consequences. We don't live in a no-fault universe. We are responsible for our behavior, and whether we like it or not, we become what we do.

The results of the rebellion are both tragic and familiar. They are tragic in the sense that human beings have successfully put asunder those things that God joined together, and they are familiar in that they describe with great accuracy the human condition as we experience it. The story describes the fragmentation in telling terms.

The "bone of my bones and flesh of my flesh" unity between the man and the woman is destroyed, and a hierarchy of power begins. "He will rule over you," says the Lord to the woman about her husband. It's worth noting that feminist complaints about patriarchal domination have ample biblical support. Such an arrangement was not part of the original design.

The symbiotic harmony between humans and the earth is the next thing to go. Abundance will no longer be automatic. "Cursed is the ground because of you; in toil you shall eat of it…thorns and thistles it shall bring forth.… By the sweat of your face you shall eat bread" (Genesis 3:17-19). It isn't hard to see the connection between the spoiling of human unity and the spoiling of the created order. Inner chaos breeds outer chaos, and until the inner unity is restored, there can be no healing of the cosmos. Paul certainly understands it in that way, and as we shall see later, he goes so far as to say that the healing of the universe is dependent upon the healing of the children of God. But that's getting ahead of our story.

The immediacy and intimacy of relationship between God and God's creatures is terminated. Adam and Eve are expelled from that environment where God walked and met them face to face, and they begin a new pilgrimage in a land where a sense of the absence of God becomes natural, and, to borrow Brother Lawrence's phrase, the presence of God is a thing that must be practiced.

Mercy is never absent from God's judgment, and the story immediately gives us two examples. The first is the "tempering of the wind to the shorn lamb," as God clothes the naked and vulnerable pair with garments made from the skins of animals. Later Jewish readers, aware of the fact that, under the Law, only the priests were permitted to wear such garments, would sense that, though Adam and Eve had become outcasts, they had not been completely stripped of their priestly dignity.

Oddly enough, the second act of mercy is the expulsion from Eden itself. You'll remember that the story names two trees set in the midst of the garden: one, the tree of the knowledge of good and evil, and the other, the tree of life. The first is the source of all the trouble, but the second promises life eternal. However, the tree of life has, by the terms of the story, ceased to be a potential blessing and is now a source of great danger to Adam and Eve. Eternal life in primal innocence would be one thing, but what if they were to eat the fruit of that tree now and be forced to live forever in their damaged and sinful condition? All of our later fictional horror stories about vampires and the undead are simply caricatures of that terrifying possibility. To live forever, with no hope of change and transformation, would be a living hell, a sentence of damnation. And so, the story says, the way back is barred by the cherubim and a flaming sword.

God's original dream has been shattered, but God is not defeated. God has better things in mind for the human race. When God curses the Serpent, whom later generations will come to identify as Satan or the Tempter, there's a promise of good things yet to come. "I will put enmity between… your offspring and hers; he will strike your head, and you will strike his heel" (Genesis 3:15). Commentators call this the *proto-evangelium,* the first hint of the gospel, with Jesus taken as the woman's seed, and the bruising of the Serpent's head as a prophecy of Satan's ultimate defeat.

Loaded with myth and metaphor, these brief accounts of our beginnings are foundational to any understanding of the rest of the Bible. They reveal a profound and primordial insight into the human condition, even as they hint at something that promises relief from our divided selves and our divided society. They encourage us to believe that a God who can create a universe by merely speaking (or, as C. S. Lewis so wondrously describes it in *The Magician's Nephew,* by singing) will not be thwarted forever. The dream of God will eventually be realized. But it will be different from the original picture. Whatever the future holds, it will not be as though the universe had not been wounded. Redeemed humanity, like the risen Christ, will bear in its body the signs of its wounding. The hope of our healing lies not in the past but in the future, and to oversimplify once again, that's what the rest of the biblical story is all about.

So I went down to the potter's house, and there he was working at his wheel. The vessel he was making of clay was spoiled in the potter's hand, and he reworked it into another vessel, as seemed good to him. Then the word of the LORD came to me: Can I not do with you, O house of Israel, just as this potter has done? says the LORD. Just like the clay in the potter's hand, so are you in my hand, O house of Israel.

—JEREMIAH 18:3-6

TWO

DAMAGE CONTROL

You Can't Go Home Again

If we were reading the story for the first time, the expulsion from the Garden of Eden would be a moment of great suspense, especially since it's followed immediately by the episode describing the birth of Adam and Eve's first offspring in which Cain races from the womb to first-degree murder in eight short verses. God has created a paradise and put people in it; he provided them with everything they needed, yet they threw it all back in his face and demanded more. The suspense would hinge on our expectations about God's response. What will he do?

Our guesses, of course, would depend largely on our assessment of God's character. So far, the story has only hinted at that. Most of what we deduce about it comes from reading ahead and then projecting back into the beginnings those insights we've gained from knowing the rest of the story.

Though the phrase "God is love" was penned by a first-generation Christian named John more than a thousand years after the writing of Genesis, and though Christians often act as if they had a patent on the notion, the words would not have come as any great surprise to the writers of the Old Testament. This deceptively simple aphorism merely puts into words what the earlier narratives describe. God's actions in the major biblical story line reveal that at the core of the universe, there beats a loving heart. And, therefore, whatever happens comes from the depths of divine love.

Admittedly, divine love sometimes looks scary. It's far tougher and more dynamic than the weak and sentimental indulgence that in many circles today masquerades as love. It seems to be more concerned with ultimate joy than with immediate pleasure. It's a love that will unrelentingly seek the good of its objects, with "good" being defined by God, not by us. What we speak of as God's wrath is simply a necessary aspect of this unremitting love. A being who could sit aloof, unmoved by injustice and human brutality, would look more like a devil than a god.

The cute little yellow buttons with the smiling face and the legend "Smile, God loves you" might be more accurate if the mouth and eyes reflected a bit more apprehension, and the message said, "Watch out! God loves you." A prominent New Testament scholar puts it this way: "The biblical story teaches us that God's love cannot be reduced to 'inclusiveness': authentic love calls us to repentance, discipline, sacrifice, and transformation."[1] The same apostolic community that proclaimed "God is love" also reminded people through another of its authors that "it is a fearful thing to fall into the hands of the living God," and "our God is a consuming fire" (Hebrews 10:31; 12:29).

Past mistakes have enduring consequences, a truth to which anyone who has lived more than a few years can bear experiential testimony. But the character of the God who invented time leads us to believe that our failings of the past need not be fatal ones, and that if we spoil Plan A, Plan B immediately becomes a viable option.

Experimentation

I once asked a world-famous physician—a man who has done extensive research into human physiology and who is a highly respected and deeply committed evangelical Christian—what he thought about the theory of evolution. His reply went something like this: "I see in nature something wonderful and marvelous. I see the hand of an amazingly creative and fertile Mind, making experiments over countless millennia, modifying them from time to time, discarding this product and that, until the desired result appears."

I thought his answer would fail to satisfy those whose view of creation comes across as bordering on the magical, where with a simple wave of a wand, a pumpkin and mice instantly become a carriage and horses ready to take Cinderella to the ball (or—as Genesis expresses it even more amazingly—with a simple spoken word, nothing instantly becomes something). Nor would it satisfy the doctrinaire evolutionist who feels compelled to insist that *only* chance and not intelligence or design is behind the universe. But it was an intriguing notion, and—disregarding the impression that God would make mistakes or fail to accomplish what he desired—there are aspects of it that square nicely with Jeremiah's image of God as the Potter.

"The vessel was spoiled in the potter's hand" is a fine summary description of the stories of Creation and Fall. What will the Potter do? The primeval *shalom* has been shattered, and the way back to Eden is barred. Can Humpty Dumpty be put together again? How will a loving God go about joining together those things that have been put asunder by our human rebellion? And if the hope of our healing lies not in the past, but in the future, which road will take us there?

The Old Testament offers us images of three possible avenues of healing, three almost archetypal remedies for ordering or correcting human behavior. These proposed panaceas appear in a variety of guises, and sometimes in combination with one another; they seem to pass in and out of fashion, but they keep reappearing. And when one proves futile, one of the other two is invariably suggested. They seem to be the natural responses of those who want to undo the evils of the past or to live in a society markedly better than the one they've inherited. At some basic level, they're probably related to our two instinctive responses to danger: flight and fight.

We might call them the Clean-Slate Approach, the Educational Approach, and the Make-'em-Do-It Approach. The biblical images for them are the Ark, the Law, and the Sword. They reflect what I will call pessimism, optimism, and imperialism. In a loose sense, the first is related to *flight,* while the other two are variations on the theme of *fight.*

Biblically, the roots of the first two may be traced back to one half of the Creation stories, and to that half's consequent assessment of human nature. Pessimism draws on the second part of the story, the part that describes the fallenness of humankind. It points to our tendency to corrupt and destroy the beauty and integrity of God's world and says, "You can't trust human nature." Optimism emphasizes the first part of the story and points to the fact that "God saw everything that he had made, and indeed, it was very good" (Genesis 1:31). It assumes that, left to ourselves, without too much outside interference, we'll probably turn out all right, and it says, "You *can* trust human nature." Imperialism assumes that the only effective way to control human nature is through the use of force, and it says, "We'll tell you who to trust."

In one variation or another they've been tried over and over again and always have been found inadequate. The most that can be said for any of them is that from time to time they offer some temporary relief, a brief respite from the problems they're meant to cure, but they always prove themselves to be incapable of offering a permanent solution. None of them is radical enough to effect systemic change—that is to say, they fail to reach the *radix,* the root of the problem. We can represent these three images by three prominent biblical characters: Noah, Moses, and David.

Intermission

A brief intermission at this point will remind us that not all biblical stories offer positive examples. Not all the prominent characters display behavior worthy of emulation, nor are all the vignettes tidy little morality tales. You don't, for example, read the story of David's buying a wife from Saul for the price of a hundred Philistine foreskins and conclude by saying, "Go and do thou likewise." Very often a biblical story offers a negative example. Paul, commenting on a disastrous episode that occurred during the Exodus, says that "these things happened to them as a warning, but they were written down for our instruction" (1 Corinthians 10:6,11, RSV).

I don't believe I'd ever given this point much thought until the time when, as a young priest, I was asked to give a talk to a gathering of Christians and Jews on the topic of brotherhood. (This sounds sexist, but that's the way we talked back in the sixties.) My natural inclination was to use a few nice biblical examples of brotherhood, but I was quickly disappointed. Obviously, Cain and Abel wouldn't do, Jacob and Esau weren't much better, and Joseph's brothers sold him into slavery. I finally copped out and talked about friendship.

The Ark

What will the Potter do? The most natural response, from a human point of view at least, is simply to start over, to take the lump of clay, ball it up, and begin again. Someone said, "If I were God, and the world had treated me the way it has treated him, I'd kick the wretched thing to pieces!" The story of Noah and the Ark is something like that. God is pictured as being pessimistic about the future of the human enterprise. He is disappointed with the results and admits to being sorry that he created the whole thing in the first place. In a poetic elaboration of the text from the medieval mystery play *Noye's Fludde,* set to music by Benjamin Britten, the voice of God thunders from offstage,

I, God, who all the world have wrought
Heaven and earth, and all of naught,

I see my people in deed and thought
Are set full foul in sin!
Man that I made I will destroy
Beast, worm, and fowl to fly
For on earth they me deny
The folk that are thereon.[2]

The experiment has gone bad, the vessel is spoiled in the Potter's hands, and seemingly the best thing to do is to start all over again. The only thing that saves humanity from total extinction is God's growing fondness for Noah and his family. Rather than create a new species, God decides to preserve the most virtuous examples of humanity and let them populate the earth again, hoping for a better result this time.

The story of the flood and the Ark has fascinated people for centuries and is one of the most widely used biblical images even today. A simple drawing of a boat with twin giraffe necks sticking up is all that you need to depict it graphically. Endless jokes have been told about the problems of keeping house on such a vessel, and about Noah's trials in finding pairs of everything. An old *New Yorker* cartoon pictures two unicorns still standing on the dock, looking wistfully at the departing vessel.

As a young man, I was much taken by Marc Connelly's play *The Green Pastures,* a work inspired by James Weldon Johnson's *God's Trombones,* in which the author tells biblical stories in the black folk idiom. The Ark episode provides a bit of comic relief at one point in which Noah reminds "de Lawd" about the dangers of snakebite and begs permission to bring along a "kag of likker." A later generation might remember a humorous Bill Cosby routine involving a conversation between God and a resistant Noah with God finally asking, "How long can you tread water?"

It may be that our often lighthearted depictions and caricatures of the incident keep something darker at bay. As anyone knows who has tried to teach young children about Noah, it is a troublesome story, concentrating as it does only on the eight survivors. What about the rest of the folk? Should we have no concern for them? Should we not weep, as the radio announcer did when the *Hindenburg* crashed and burned, "Oh, the humanity!" No honest dramatic presentation of the story can ignore the anguish and the suffering of those who must have suddenly realized that it really was too late and that they had no more second chances. All of their opportunities for repentance had expired, and they had been left behind to perish. Irrevocable abandonment by God is the stuff of nightmares. "Abandon hope" indeed! We instinctively long for a larger ark. But that's getting ahead of the story.

The tale of the Ark is the first in a long series of survival tales about how to preserve the human race in the event of impending catastrophe. Modern variations, usually involving a nuclear holocaust or a cataclysmic collision with a comet or asteroid, suggest that the select few might be shielded from destruction by hiding in "the dens and caves of the earth," underground shelters, or even in spaceships touring the galaxy while the rest of humanity perishes. In all such stories, the hope is invariably voiced that, with a new beginning, things will be different. The humans will learn from the mistakes of the past, and having been made wiser by their ordeal, they will do a better job in the future. The Ark is the equivalent of the shelter, the spaceship, in which the first generation of a new society will build a brave new world after the old one has perished through its own folly.

The only problem is that it doesn't work. Just as in the other survival stories, we know that good intentions won't get the job done, and we almost unconsciously wait for the other shoe to drop, for a crack to develop in the protagonists' facade of virtue. God makes a covenant with Noah, seals it with a rainbow, and vows not to curse the earth ever again, but it isn't long before Noah is drunk and disorderly (his "kag of likker"?), his conduct has shamed his children, and he has cursed one of his grandchildren. The cycle of sin begins again. The repetitious nature of our rebellion is signaled by the story that immediately follows. The erection of the Tower of Babel is one more attempt to "snatch at equality with God," to "make a name for ourselves," rather than to be content with the name God gives.

What happened? In *The Green Pastures,* Noah tells God, in a winsome phrase, "I ain' very much, Lawd, but I'se all I got." Who among us could say anything more eloquent? The problem is that there's more truth to the statement than this fictional Noah imagined. The best of what we might call "natural goodness" is still too closely related to Adam and Eve. Its DNA is the same, still damaged and distorted, and the best of human beings, left on their own, will continue to repeat the errors of the past. Human nature *is* evenly distributed.

The Ark, then, becomes an ambiguous and ambivalent symbol. On the positive side it's a type or image of the many intentional communities that, over the centuries, have been formed to preserve the light in the face of overwhelming darkness. The desire to live a virtuous life has led many people to disassociate themselves from what they consider to be a corrupt society or church and live apart in isolated companies of the faithful. Pessimistic about the possibility of effecting any real change in their surrounding culture, they have banded together with other like-minded individuals with the intention of preserving a way of life that they see crumbling all around them. A century and a half before the days of Jesus, a group of pious Jews, feeling that the temple worship in Jerusalem had been defiled, fled to the desert at Qumran, near the Dead Sea, hoping to become the saving remnant of their people. Some Christians of the early centuries did much the same thing, retreating to the isolation of the Egyptian desert or to small monastic communities on the European continent.

Many of these people lived exemplary lives, encouraged by images of the Ark, and by remembering that the people of Israel had been formed and instructed while in the desert, isolated from contact with the larger human community. The world owes a great debt to these saving remnants, these small visionary elites who have modeled for us those good things that we've been unwilling or unable to do for ourselves. The courage and foresight of faithful people to "build an ark" in the face of impending disaster, to face an uncertain future with the bravado of "We few, we happy few, we band of brothers" have left us an enduring legacy. The Celtic monks of the British isles, the Benedictines and Franciscans of Italy, and countless other communities kept the torch of mission and learning alive during many perilous centuries. Perhaps most important of all, they became the repositories of our most precious possessions. The Qumran community preserved for us those invaluable documents known as the Dead Sea Scrolls. The later Christian communities preserved the Scriptures, our corporate memory.

The dark side of the Ark, indeed of any intentional community, appears when its members forget their own feet of clay and assume that their privileged position among the saved makes them immune to ordinary human failings. Paul reminded a particularly smug group of first-century Christians, "If you think you are standing, watch out that you do not fall" (1 Corinthians 10:12). A saving remnant ceases to have the ability to save when its constituents become so conscious of their own virtue that they begin to look with disdain on those outside their fellowship. When the gathering becomes the holy huddle of the "saved" and can no longer shed a tear, much less toss out a lifeline to those who are perishing, it fails in its original purpose.

The desire to get rid of troublemakers is probably universal. In virtually any community there are always those members we feel we could do better without. Thank God we don't generally act on our feelings, but the temptation is still there. I've known many clergy who, only half in jest, have said that there are no problems in their congregation that a few well-chosen funerals wouldn't solve. Pessimism about the ability of others to change is usually accompanied by a measurable degree of blindness to one's own faults.

Many years ago I had the privilege of participating in a small prayer and fellowship group in a local parish. The people involved had authentic and powerful encounters with the living God, and as a result, their lives were noticeably different from what they'd been before. In the early stages they were awestruck by the experience and viewed themselves as undeserving recipients of unexpected and amazing gifts of grace. Then some began to see themselves as bearers of a precious gift to their fellow parishioners, as a saving remnant within their own parish. Finally, a few began to look down on those outside their own small community, those who hadn't shared in their particular experience of God's power. Before the year was out, one of its members approached me and said, "Bishop, it's time to draw the line at St. Blank's. We have to find out who's with the Lord and who isn't." I thought for a moment, then replied, "And if we had drawn that line twelve months ago, which side would you have been on?" His response—the only proper one under the circumstances—was a shamefaced "Oops!"

Denominational divisions are frequently led by ark builders who fear a future inundation, forgetting the rainbow promise that "never again shall all flesh be cut off by the waters of a flood" (Genesis 9:11).

The Law

The second approach to healing the damage done in Eden is the Law. The Ark was only temporarily successful, since the survivors turned out to be pretty much like their ancestors. If the Ark represented flight from the evil of the world, the Law implies a fight. Sin will be dealt with by the revelation of a divine code of conduct. If the Ark represents pessimism, the Law represents a form of optimism. It's an early form of "salvation by education." Reveal the Law, it seems to say, and people will obey it.

When the Bible speaks of the Law—the Torah—it isn't referring simply to the Ten Commandments, nor even to the many other rules and regulations, some ceremonial, some moral and ethical, that the Bible contains. The Torah refers to all of the first five books of the Bible. The Commandments are only part of the Torah, but the "Ten Words," as they're generally called by Jewish scholars, symbolize the Law as no other passage can.

"The sheer brilliance of the Ten Commandments is that they codify in a handful of words acceptable human behavior, not just for then or now, but for all time. Language evolves. Power shifts from one nation to another. Messages are transmitted with the speed of light. Man erases one frontier after another. And yet we and our behavior and the commandments governing that behavior remain the same," said television journalist Ted Koppel in his 1987 commencement address at Duke University.[3]

In a similar vein, Thomas Cahill says, "They require no justification, nor can they be argued away. They are not dependent on circumstances, nor may they be set aside because of special considerations. They are not propositions for debate. They are not suggestions. They are not even (as a recent book would have us imagine in the jargon of our day) 'ten challenges.' They are exactly what they seem to be."[4]

In the saga of the Exodus, the anthropomorphic picture of God is a bit more muted than in the Creation narratives. Outside Eden, it seems, God no longer speaks face to face with his chosen ones, but there's direct communication nonetheless. From the bush that burns but isn't consumed comes the voice of God. God reveals both his name and his modus operandi to Moses during this brief encounter. "I have observed the misery of my people who are in Egypt; I have heard their cry on account of their taskmasters. Indeed, I know their sufferings, and I have come down to deliver them from the Egyptians, and to bring them up out of that land to a good and broad land, a land flowing with milk and honey," says the Lord (Exodus 3:7-8). God sees, God hears, God knows, and God comes to rescue. Four verbs define "God is love" for Moses. This is not the God of the philosophers exercising a remote and passive beneficence, but the God of Creation, demonstrating for all time a passionate love that is active and involved in the lives of those who are its objects.

As in the story of the Ark, safe passage through the waters is the mark of a new beginning for God's chosen ones. And as in the story of the Ark, the wicked perish in the sea.

The Passover liturgy, with its recitation of, "We were slaves in Egypt and God with his mighty outstretched arm set us free," testifies to the centrality of this event for Jewish identity. It's the Jewish "Declaration of Interdependence," and as such, it is not complete until the covenant has been sealed with the Ten Words. They are the sign of the divine-human covenant, the most precious treasure of the chosen people.

What would it be like to hear this story for the first time? What would it be like to watch your leader begin the climb to the top of the mountain, shrouded in clouds, with thunder and lightning shaking the earth, there to hear the voice of God himself, the Lord who has descended from heaven to meet with his chosen representative? Fear, wonder, and a spine-tingling expectancy would be appropriate. Will our apparently aimless wanderings in the desert now come to an end? Will we finally discover the true meaning of life?

The visual images and the dramatic possibilities inherent in the Exodus story are stunning, and they haven't been lost on our modern mythmakers in Hollywood. *The Ten Commandments* and *The Prince of Egypt* bear ample testimony to the raw power of the biblical story.

I have often wondered if Steven Spielberg was consciously remythologizing the Bible when he captured something of these dramatic possibilities in the final scenes of *Close Encounters of the Third Kind*. The setting could have been taken straight from the pages of Exodus. It was all there—a mountain with access prohibited to all except the chosen, the dazzling chandelier-like spaceship descending with whirling clouds and thunder and brilliant light, and mysterious beings of light who have come ostensibly for the purpose of revealing to poor benighted human beings the "secrets of the universe." Our optimism waits with breathless expectation in the presence of these superior beings whose civilization and technology are literally light-years beyond ours. It says, "Tell us these secrets and we will be satisfied, and our world will be transformed from darkness into light."

And what are these "secrets of the universe"? Are they, as T. S. Eliot once described it, "systems so perfect that no one will have to be good"? Probably not. Superior science may advance our technology, but it leaves our humanity untouched. On Sinai, the awesome secret of the universe is simply, "I am the LORD your God.... You shall have no other gods before me" (Exodus 20:2-3, NIV).

The Ten Words probably contained few surprises for the people of Israel. After all, they're hardly utopian, nor are they the outlandish inventions of some capricious deity. They're the simple and basic essentials for the ordering of any human society. How to hold it together; what to do until Messiah comes. They are words that strike a responsive chord deep inside us where the image and likeness of God has not been completely destroyed through our rebellion.

If there's any problem with the Law, it isn't to be found in the Law's content—that is indisputable. The problem, as the story itself eventually reveals, is the Law's inability to produce the sort of society it envisions. It can describe righteous behavior, but by itself it does not produce righteousness. Why? When we're being honest with ourselves, we must admit that the very notion of Law, a set of rules and regulations for our conduct, reveals how deeply wedded we still are to our first ancestors. A simple "Thou shalt," or "Thou shalt not" produces an almost instinctive reaction of, "Oh yeah? Sez who?" Our inner longing to be as gods and our desire for autonomy are very strong. We aren't as far removed from our rebellious ancestors as we might like to believe.

Before Moses had returned from the mountaintop, the people of Israel had persuaded Aaron to make other gods for them, and they began to dance around a golden calf. Their problem, like ours, was not ignorance but impotence. It was G. K. Chesterton who reminded us that the ways of God have "not been tried and found wanting, but found to be difficult and not tried." Like us, the Israelites found the biblical God too awesome and exacting, and as a result, they established that still-vigorous cottage industry of manufacturing designer gods more in keeping with their own desires.

The Law should serve as a haunting reminder that knowledge and education, however desirable they may be, do not by themselves solve the problems of our society and our world. The temptation is great, when we're faced with some form of social evil, to pass a new law prohibiting it or to mount a massive educational program to unmask its destructive effects. Legalism can be very attractive. An obvious example is the fact that decades of educational programs and hundreds of statutes, laws, and prohibitions have stemmed neither the flow of illegal drugs nor their use by millions of people. We deceive ourselves if we think that by having passed laws and raised public awareness, we've solved the problem. The laws and the campaigns are not wrong, but *by themselves* they lack the element most needed: the power to transform.

The biblical story reminds us that, over and over again, God's people swear allegiance to the Law and to the covenants that God makes with them, and over and over again they "forget the Lord and do what is evil in his sight." For all its brilliance, the Law is still written on tablets of stone where it remains external to the world's great superpower, the human heart. But the biblical story is not without hope. The prophets of Israel, contemplating this very thing, hear the Lord speak of a future time when,

> I will make a new covenant with the house of Israel and the house of Judah. It will not be like the covenant that I made with their ancestors when I took them by the hand to bring them out of the land of Egypt—a covenant that they broke, though I was their husband, says the LORD. But this is the covenant that I will make with the house of Israel after those days, says the LORD: *I will put my law within them, and I will write it on their hearts;* and I will be their God, and they shall be my people. No longer shall they teach one another, or say to each other, "Know the LORD," for they shall all know me, from the least of them to the greatest, says the LORD; for I will forgive their iniquity, and remember their sin no more. (Jeremiah 31:31-34)

And,

> I shall give you a new heart and put a new spirit within you; I shall remove the heart of stone from your body and give you a heart of flesh. I shall put my spirit within you and make you conform to my statutes; you will observe my laws faithfully.... You will be my people, and I shall be your God. (Ezekiel 36:26-28, REB)

The finger of God, which on Sinai carved the Ten Words on tablets of stone, isn't finished yet. There's more to come.

The Sword

When people want to ridicule the Bible, they never begin by mocking "God is love" or the Ten Commandments. They don't complain about the Sermon on the Mount, the Golden Rule, the prodigal son, the good Samaritan, or Paul's great hymn about love in the thirteenth chapter of 1 Corinthians.

No, the target of opportunity is usually the violence and the bloodshed, the tales of countless battles and wholesale slaughter that occupy so much space in the historical books of the Old Testament. And hostile critics are not the only problem. I have occasionally found myself in an awkward moral dilemma when, during a church service, a lector finishes one of these passages, such as one calling for the destruction of the Canaanites, "man and woman, infant and suckling, ox and sheep, camel and ass" (1 Samuel 15:3, KJV), by saying, "The word of the Lord." The correct liturgical response is, "Thanks be to God!" But even as I automatically parrot the words, I wonder if it makes me an accomplice to genocide.

The wild fertility rites and infant sacrifices of many of the conquered tribes, the brutal excesses of the primitive warring clans, the political coverups and inflated accounts of the bravery of the conquerors and the numbers of the vanquished are beyond the scope of this book. I refer to them only as symbolizing the fact that when reason and law fail, the use of force is invariably our court of last resort. Indeed, since neither the Ark nor the Law was capable of undoing the damage inflicted in Eden, the biblical story recounts in savage detail the exploits of champions and kings who through military force sought to impose on others the kingdom of God— or at least the power of God's people. At certain critical times God authorized and even initiated military action (as in Deuteronomy 7:1-2; 20:10-18; Joshua 10:40-42; 11:20-23; and 1 Samuel 15:2-3), but some went beyond this. Today we call it imperialism, and it's still alive and well.

In the people's response to God's repeated command to "go in and possess the land" he had given them, many of the battles were land grabs, pure and simple, while some were defensive in nature. The particular piece of real estate the Israelites inherited from God lay on a major trade route, and traveling armies often had little better to do than try to knock off a few Jews and pick up whatever booty they could find as they passed through the Holy Land. The current hostilities in the Middle East seem to be the prolongation of wars that are thousands of years old.

These violent episodes undoubtedly served as inspiration for the imperialistic attempts of a medieval Christianity to impose itself by force on those who did not believe. I have a wonderful cartoon depicting a large medieval army, with catapults and battering rams, encamped outside a walled city. The army's leader says to a man on the wall, "We've come to talk to you about Jesus." It was meant to be a humorous dig at what some people call "terrorist evangelism," the kind of thing you experience when an overly zealous Christian pins you against a wall and won't let you go until you've recited the proper formula of Christian belief.

I thought the cartoon was funny when I first saw it, but I have to confess that my laughter was somewhat muted when I recalled that, back in the Middle Ages, a number of bishops kept their own standing armies. (Now *there's* an idea!) It's a little dangerous to laugh when you remember that we're among those wonderful people who produced the Crusades, the Inquisition, and the conquistadors.

Aberrations such as these are vivid illustrations of the universality of human nature, and they remind us of Lord Acton's observation that power corrupts, and absolute power corrupts absolutely. The biblical accounts of the use of the Sword are not unaware of this truism, and the stories occasionally reflect it. As in the accounts of the Ark and the Law, they tend to be a bit ambivalent.

On the one hand, the stories sometimes appear to glorify bloodshed and battle, but on the other hand, we have the strange case of David, the "man after God's own heart." Beloved David, the legendary warrior-king, who successfully united all of Israel and became his nation's archetypal hero through his fierce devotion to God and his military prowess, was, toward the end of his life, forbidden to fulfill his heart's desire to build a temple for the Lord because of the very battles he had fought in the Lord's name. He was told he had too much blood on his hands. The task of building the temple would fall instead to his son, whose name was a variant of *shalom*, Solomon.

However you wish to interpret this part of the biblical narrative— whether you revel in the audacity and courage of the warriors or lament the fact that the people of God could indulge in such shameful behavior—the fact remains that the Sword, like the Ark and the Law, eventually failed. As we said in the last chapter, the one thing the omnipotent God most desires—the free and loving response of the human heart—is something that cannot be secured by an exercise of power.

At the end of the story, after the dust of all the battles has settled and all the bodies have been buried, the kingdom of God has not been established. Solomon's temple has been desecrated and destroyed, the holy city of Jerusalem laid waste, and its residents scattered to the four winds as refugees or captives.

To use a more modern example, World War II did indeed halt the onslaught of a demonic Nazism, but it did not bring about true peace. Witness the fifty years of the Cold War and the ethnic and nationalistic violence that has erupted after its demise. The *shalom* of God cannot be established by something that is its very antithesis.

Here again, however, the Bible speaks a word of hope. Both Micah and Isaiah hear identical words from God, words that seem to reflect not only God's judgment on the sword, but a promise of a nonviolent future.

In days to come
    the mountain of the LORD's house
shall be established as the highest of the mountains,
    and shall be raised above the hills;
all the nations shall stream to it.
    Many peoples shall come and say,
"Come, let us go up to the mountain of the LORD,
    to the house of the God of Jacob;
that he may teach us his ways
    and that we may walk in his paths."
For out of Zion shall go forth instruction,
    and the word of the LORD from Jerusalem.
He shall judge between the nations,
    and shall arbitrate for many peoples;
they shall beat their swords into plowshares,
    and their spears into pruning hooks;
nation shall not lift up sword against nation,
    neither shall they learn war any more. (Isaiah 2:2-4; see also
        Micah 4:1-3)

Parenthetically, I was asked to preach one Sunday at the Air Force Academy in Colorado Springs, a day when the appointed Old Testament lesson was this very passage. What could I say to career military people to help them respond to these powerful words from Isaiah? I wasn't unaware that protesters regularly gathered at the gates of the academy to denounce the "warmongering of the military industrial complex," nor was I unaware that at least some military chaplains had given the impression that the Bible's commands about killing may be set aside when "the national interest" is at stake. Neither of these approaches seemed helpful, so I finally wound up reminding my listeners of another prophetic passage that speaks of a time when all will know the Lord and there will no longer be a need for preachers. "Since both of us are in what the Bible says are diminishing professions," I said, "the sooner we both work ourselves out of a job, the better." They seemed to agree.

Four Gifts

Elie Wiesel, the great Jewish poet, philosopher, and survivor of the Holocaust, has spoken about four gifts that Judaism has given to the world: "a unitive view of Creation, a linear understanding of history, the centrality of justice, and Messianism."[5] The Genesis story of our origins bears eloquent testimony to the "unitive view of Creation." Human beings are brought forth from the dust of the earth, or as one modern liturgy puts it, "From the primal elements you brought forth the human race, and blessed us with memory, reason, and skill."[6]

The story also points to the necessity of the second gift. Because we take it for granted, we often overlook this most revolutionary claim of biblical faith, the notion that history is linear. It has a beginning and an ending. The story of life is not, as virtually all the primitive religions would have it, cyclical. To quote Thomas Cahill again,

> In the revolving drama of the heavens, primitive peoples saw an immortal, wheel-like pattern that was predictive of mortal life....
> The spiral, ever turning, ever beginning again, is the image of the cyclical nature of reality—of the phases of the moon, the changing of the seasons, the cycle of a woman's body, the ever turning Wheel of birth, copulation, and death.[7]

The biblical story changed all that. It isn't about a Disneyfied "circle of life," nor is it a fairy tale in which God simply declares "All is forgiven," and

everyone lives happily ever after. There may be strong mythological elements in the biblical story, but they are *serious* myth. They reveal the truth.
The way back to Eden is barred, and the story can only go forward. We
pass this way but once, and our stories have a beginning and an ending. As
we saw earlier, it isn't a no-fault universe, and actions have consequences.
Life is very real, and reality bites.

The third gift in Wiesel's list, the centrality of justice, is linked to those
same stories, since the idyllic picture of Eden—God's original dream of the
peaceable kingdom—is the very essence of justice and shalom. It also finds
expression in the Law, and no understanding of the Old Testament is complete without it. As the extension of the Law, another of God's pictures of
what true justice looks like, it's the common burden of all the prophets.
Their message was always a call to "look to the rock from which you were
hewn," an exhortation to remember the early covenants through which
God sought to establish a just society, a world in which the operating prin-
ciple is the original shalom described in Genesis.

Wiesel's fourth point was Messianism—the hope of a coming redemption through the offices of a promised Anointed One. Messianic hope testifies to trust in the promises of God, to an awareness that God hasn't
yet finished what he began. The Old Testament ends on a note of "to be
continued."

Neither the Ark nor the Law nor the Sword has been capable of undoing the damage done in Eden. The clay hasn't yet become what the Potter
envisioned. There's something else yet to be accomplished. What will it be?
After the Ark, God promises that he'll never forget his people; after the Law,
God promises to write it in our hearts; and after the Sword, God promises a
peaceful future. Finally, an even better promise is made, one that seems to
say that, in view of all that has gone before, something entirely different must
be tried. In Isaiah we read a promise of a radically new beginning, so radical
that it can only be described as a second Genesis, an entirely new creation:

For I am about to create new heavens
　　and a new earth;
the former things shall not be remembered
　　or come to mind.
But be glad and rejoice forever
　　in what I am creating....
I will rejoice in Jerusalem,
　　and delight in my people;
no more shall the sound of weeping be heard in it,
　　or the cry of distress....
They shall not labor in vain,
　　or bear children for calamity....
Before they call I will answer,
　　while they are yet speaking I will hear.
The wolf and the lamb shall feed together,
　　the lion shall eat straw like the ox;
　　but the serpent—its food shall be dust!
They shall not hurt or destroy
　　on all my holy mountain,
　　says the LORD. (Isaiah 65:17-19,23-25)

Wiesel speaks of "Messianism." One theologian remarked that the Bible contains "an excess of promise." There's more promised in the Scriptures, he said, than has yet been fulfilled. It begs for a second volume. Another theologian puts it another way: "There is an *overdose of hope* in the history of promise that drives both Israel and the church to be moving forward restlessly with an incurable case of 'messianitis.'"[8]

Indeed, the story is to be continued, but it will be continued with an "overdose of hope," a hope that enables us to hear the melody of the future. The Potter has one more plan for the clay.

Jesus not only teaches us the Christian life; He creates it in our souls by the action of His Spirit. Our life in Him is not a matter of mere ethical goodwill. It is not a mere moral perfection. It is an entirely new spiritual reality, an inner transformation.

—THOMAS MERTON

For as in Adam all die, even so in Christ shall all be made alive.

—1 CORINTHIANS 15:22, KJV

O God of unchangeable power and eternal light: Look favorably on your whole Church, that wonderful and sacred mystery; by the effectual working of your providence, carry out in tranquillity the plan of salvation; let the whole world see and know that things which were cast down are being raised up, and things which had grown old are being made new, and that all things are being brought to their perfection by him through whom all things were made, your Son Jesus Christ our Lord. Amen.

—BOOK OF COMMON PRAYER

THREE

ONCE MORE, FROM THE BEGINNING

Using the New Lens

It's time to place the Creation lens over the gospel story and see what it reveals. And one of the first things we need to look for is the identity of the principal character.

When we have a new experience and try to describe it to others, we usually do it in terms of something we've known or experienced before. We try to find some common ground that will enable our listeners to grasp what we're trying to say. "It reminded me of the time when…," or "She looked a lot like Aunt Helen," or "It tasted something like cinnamon."

Two thousand years ago, a small group of people had the unique opportunity of being in close contact with an itinerant Jewish rabbi named Jesus. The impact on their lives was cosmic. They were overwhelmed by his personality, by his teaching, by the ways in which he interacted with both the great and the small, by his life, his death, and even more powerfully, by his resurrection. The experience turned their lives not upside down but right side up.

How could they possibly describe all of this to other people? To what or to whom could they compare him? As people rooted in the Scriptures, steeped in the history and tradition of their nation's past, they had a wealth of personalities and stories to serve as models or metaphors.

They could have said that he was like a great patriarch, a second Abraham who would be the father of a large family with heirs as countless as the stars in the heavens. Or he might have been likened to the great lawgiver, a second Moses, come to reassert and fine-tune the Torah. He might have been compared to one of the prophets, a second Elijah or Isaiah or Jeremiah. Though his battles seemed to be with spiritual rather than political enemies, he could have been thought of as a second David, a new warrior-king. Or he might have been likened to the wisest of them all, a second Solomon.

But, in fact, they discovered that none of these descriptions were adequate to the task, and in every context where such names are mentioned, Jesus is found to be superior to all of them. He is "worthy of much more glory than Moses," he is "greater than Solomon," and he is "before Abraham" (Hebrews 3:3; Matthew 12:42; John 8:58). Elijah has already come, in the person of John the Baptizer, and has borne witness to Jesus, saying that he is "not worthy to untie…his sandals" (Luke 3:16). David, in the Psalms, calls him "Lord."

Instead, he is called a second *Adam,* a name that takes us back to the very beginning of Creation. Paul is the one who provides the description, although, as we'll see, the notion behind the description is found throughout the New Testament. "Adam," he said, "is a type of the one who was to come" (Romans 5:14). "Thus it is written, 'The first man, Adam, became a living being'; the last Adam became a life-giving spirit" (1 Corinthians 15:45). And along with this description comes an astounding promise: "Just as we have borne the image of the man of dust, we will also bear the image of the man of heaven" (1 Corinthians 15:49).

Paul was a preacher, a master of the spoken word. He was not like

today's preachers, with ready-made congregations and a choir seated behind or to one side of the pulpit. But he did a lot of talking. Language was
his stock in trade. The sparse records we have of his preaching indicate that
he spoke to a wide variety of audiences, from small gatherings of intense
Jewish believers in a synagogue to a polytheistic mob of Athenians on Mars
Hill.

Like all preachers, he utilized images, scriptural texts, metaphors, stories, and illustrations that he found helpful in getting his message across.
And like all preachers, he used them over and over again, sometimes modifying and remolding them for a particular audience or a unique set of circumstances. His letters form only a small part of his preaching, but as we
read them we get glimpses of the basic message he was trying to get across.
We can begin to discern the thought patterns that shaped what he said and
almost re-create the sermon notes scribbled on the back of a parchment
envelope and carried in the pocket of his toga. One thing emerges almost
immediately. As Paul reflected on Jesus, he only twice referred to what Jesus
said,[1] preferring instead to concentrate on who Jesus *is* and what Jesus *did*.
He would not have understood our fascination with red-letter editions of
the New Testament that highlight only the *words* of Jesus.

He may have been reflecting on the "excess of promise" and the "overdose of hope" mentioned in the last chapter, when he told the church in
Corinth that in Jesus, "every one of God's promises is a 'Yes' " (2 Corinthians 1:20). One translation is even more graphic: "He is the Yes pronounced
upon God's promises, every one of them" (NEB). Even allowing for a little
bit of preacher's hyperbole, that is a stunning statement, and it offers an
important clue to Paul's understanding of Jesus. Paul's words are, after all,
simply the outward and visible sign of his deepest inward and spiritual convictions, and they inevitably raise the question, "What must he have believed in order to say what he said?"

The Image Behind the Words

First of all, Paul believed that God's promises to never forget his people, to write the Law in their hearts, and to abolish the sword as a means of accomplishing his purposes, all find their fulfillment in Jesus. And even more radical, Paul seemed to be convinced that the promise of a new heaven and a new earth, of a brand-new beginning for the human race, has already begun to come true.

He described it as a "new creation." And although he used the phrase only twice, it is evident that the image behind the phrase permeated a great deal of his thought. It's a metaphor, of course, but for Paul it was a very prominent metaphor, and one he took seriously and used widely. It was as though God had decided that humanity's disease was too far advanced to be cured, and since the infection was universal, there were no healthy specimens left who could serve as the pioneers of a new future, the Adam and Eve of a new race. As a result, God had gone back to the very beginning and once again had uttered the divine fiat, "Let there be light." Or, as Paul put it, "It is the God who said, 'Let light shine out of darkness,' who has shone in our hearts to give the light of the knowledge of the glory of God in the face of Jesus Christ" (2 Corinthians 4:6). The promise of new heavens and a new earth was beginning to be fulfilled.

Paul was not alone in his convictions. Judging from the written record of the fledgling Christian community, Paul's interpretation was not unique but typical. Although other writers may have expressed it differently, the same image and perception of what God was doing in Jesus can be seen as the background of their words.

For example, one of the first things you notice when you read the New Testament through the Creation lens is the large number of things that are described as "new." There are references to new wine, new teaching, new tongues, new covenant, new commandment, new life, new humanity, new creation, new self, new way, new birth, new heavens and a new earth, new name, and a new Jerusalem, all of which seem to culminate in the declaration of the One "that sat upon the throne... Behold, I make all things new" (Revelation 21:5, KJV). There's an inescapable sense that, in response to God's promises, what had been considered to be an event reserved for some remote future is already breaking into the present. The New Testament writers seemed to sense that God was offering a brand-new start to the human race, one that was so radically different from the earlier ones that it almost defied description.

An account in our local newspaper tells of the discovery of some ancient rock paintings in western Texas. Photographs of apparently empty rock faces, when viewed through a particular filtering lens, revealed that the rocks were covered with complex artistic designs. In a similar fashion, the Creation lens, added to the Salvation lens and the Pneumatic lens, reveals facets of the Christian story that we don't usually see, and like a holograph, it makes that story three dimensional.

One of the first gifts of the risen Christ to his disciples was to open the Scriptures for them, to enable them to read those familiar words as through a new lens, and in so doing, to open their hearts and minds to understand those Scriptures in a fresh way.

New Creation and a New Adam

While the phrase "new creation" is uniquely Pauline, the image itself is virtually everywhere in the New Testament. Writing to the Corinthians, Paul refers to God's command to "let light shine out of darkness," then he goes on to speak of what happens when people enter into union with the risen Christ. The sentence in the original Greek is an elliptical one and can best be translated, "United to Christ—New Creation!" It's his way of saying two things. First, that the Christian life is more than a matter of affiliation with a new group of people, though it is that, and it's more than a new allegiance to a set of principles, though it is that, too. It's more like the fusing of personalities. We enter into the very life of Christ, or as Thomas Merton describes it, "It is an entirely new spiritual reality, an inner transformation." And second, that when we do that, God begins to unleash within us the same power that brought the universe into being. Paul has been accused of many things, but never of timidity of expression!

He was not ignorant of the mystery and beauty of the created universe. The words of the psalmist were very familiar to him: "When I consider thy heavens, the work of thy fingers, the moon and the stars, which thou hast ordained; what is man, that thou art mindful of him?" (Psalm 8:3-4, KJV). His understanding of the new creation is soaked in the same sense of awe.

A number of old familiar Christian hymns have picked up this Creation imagery. Samuel J. Stone's "The Church's One Foundation" says of the church, "She is his new creation by water and the word." Charles Wesley's "Love Divine" asks God to "Finish, then, thy new creation; pure and spotless let us be." And Walter Russell Bowie's more recent "Lord Christ, when first thou cam'st to earth" ends with the cry, "O wounded hands of Jesus, build in us thy new creation."[2]

When Paul described the entry of Jesus into the human predicament, in writing to the church in Philippi, his mind seemed to go back to the opening chapters of Genesis:

> Let the same mind be in you that was in Christ Jesus,
>   who, though he was in the form of God,
>   did not regard equality with God
>   as something to be exploited,
>   but emptied himself,
>   taking the form of a slave,

being born in human likeness.
And being found in human form,
>he humbled himself
>and became obedient to the point of death—
>even death on a cross. (Philippians 2:5-8)

The imagery is clear and again reveals Paul's convictions about what God is doing in Jesus. Adam and Eve, though human, sought to snatch at equality with God, to "become as gods." But the Second Adam, reversing the action, seeks to undo the deep and far-reaching results of that first rebellion. Paul, writing to the church in Galatia, described some of the effects of that reversal:

As many of you as were baptized into Christ have clothed yourselves with Christ. There is no longer Jew or Greek, there is no longer slave or free, there is no longer male and female; for all of you are one in Christ Jesus. (Galatians 3:27-28)

Sin brought us separation and alienation, both from God and from all other human beings. But in the new creation, the spiritual, racial, economic, and sexual chasms are being bridged, and there are fresh possibilities open to those who seek to share life with Jesus. The grace of God does not rewrite history—what's done is done. But that grace is able to begin to heal the wounds of our history and to offer us a foretaste of the promised future shalom where all will be reconciled.

In the Gospels

One of the first hints of the Second Adam image in the Gospels is found in Luke's description of the Annunciation:

In the sixth month the angel Gabriel was sent by God to a town in Galilee called Nazareth, to a virgin engaged to a man whose name was Joseph, of the house of David. The virgin's name was Mary. And he came to her and said, "Greetings, favored one! The Lord is with you." But she was much perplexed by his words and pondered what sort of greeting this might be. The angel said to her, "Do not be afraid, Mary, for you have found favor with God. And now, you will conceive in your womb and bear a son, and you will name him Jesus. He will be great, and will be called the Son of the Most High…and of his kingdom there will be no end." Mary said to the angel, "How can this be, since I am a virgin?" The angel said to her, "The Holy Spirit will come upon you, and the power of the Most High will overshadow you; therefore the child to be born will be holy; he will be called Son of God…for nothing will be impossible with God." Then Mary said, "Here am I, the servant of the Lord; let it be with me according to your word." Then the angel departed from her. (Luke 1:26-38)

As Luke reflects on Mary's story (where else could it have come from?), he seems to sense a recapitulation of the Genesis story of the creation of the first Adam, but with a major difference. In response to Mary's natural question, "How can this be?" the angel tells her of the overshadowing power of God's Spirit. The same *ruach* (Spirit) that in the beginning overshadowed the face of the waters, the same breath (Spirit) that God blew into his lifeless creature of dust in order that Adam might become "a living being" will breathe into Mary's womb, and the Second Adam will be conceived.

But in this Creation story, there's a crucial difference. After his explanation, Gabriel appears to pause. It's a pause that seems to bring the whole of creation to a momentary standstill, for his words carry an unspoken invitation, and until Mary responds, everything else is on hold. "These things" *cannot* be without the sovereign intervention of God. But they *will not* be without human assent. God intends to begin a new creation, but God stoops to request our participation. (That pattern of divine power waiting upon human permission, or in many cases, human petition, holds true in all of our encounters with the living God.)

What powerful eloquence comes from the lips of an awestruck young Jewish girl! "Here am I, the servant of the Lord; let it be with me according to your word" (Luke 1:38). Small wonder that Mary has been called the model Christian. With her reply, the rhythm of the universe resumes, but with a difference. Nothing will ever be the same again.

Like Paul, Luke is convinced that the new creation can begin only with a new type of human being, one "conceived by the power of the Holy Spirit, and born of the Virgin Mary." Unaided, human nature has long proved to be inadequate for anything except brief episodic attempts at unity with God's purposes. Nothing less than incarnation—humanity invaded by God's own being—will be capable of getting the job done.

Another new creation clue is found in all three Synoptic Gospels. Matthew, Mark, and Luke all witness to Jesus' struggle with Satan—the devil—in the wilderness, reminiscent of the first humans' encounter with the Tempter in Eden. A careful reading of the temptations reveals that Satan has no new tricks up his sleeve but simply offers variations on his original theme—hunger, power, and rivalry with God. And when we read this story and hear Jesus' rebuttals, the inference is obvious—wisdom *doesn't* grow on trees, and the ending of *this* story will be quite different from the ending of the first one. The Second Adam has proved to be more adept at dealing with temptation than the first.

John, a Second Genesis

But the most striking reflection of the new creation and Second Adam imagery is found in John's gospel. We don't have to place our Creation lens over his account because John has done it already. Without too much exaggeration, John might be called "Genesis in the New Testament." His opening words, "In the beginning," are a dead giveaway:

> In the beginning was the Word, and the Word was with God, and the Word was God. He was in the beginning with God. All things came into being through him, and without him not one thing came into being. What has come into being in him was life, and the life was the light of all people. The light shines in the darkness, and the darkness did not overcome it.
>
> There was a man sent from God, whose name was John. He came as a witness to testify to the light, so that all might believe through him. He himself was not the light, but he came to testify to the light. The true light, which enlightens everyone, was coming into the world.
>
> He was in the world, and the world came into being through him; yet the world did not know him. He came to what was his own, and his own people did not accept him. But to all who received him, who believed in his name, he gave power to become children of God, who were born, not of blood or of the will of the flesh or of the will of man, but of God.
>
> And the Word became flesh and lived among us, and we have seen his glory, the glory as of a father's only son, full of grace and truth. (John 1:1-14)

Genesis tells us about the creation of the universe, but John reveals a detail that Genesis omitted—the creative Word, the Agent of Creation. And even as he does so, you can sense that John is struggling with a deep theological dilemma. As a devout Jew, he is unswervingly committed to the unity of God. The *Shema,* the Jewish creed, says, "Hear, O Israel, the Lord our God, the Lord is one." And so John stretches his language to the breaking point to say something that perhaps he himself cannot fully comprehend. "The Word was with God, and the Word was God. He was in the beginning with God." God is one, and yet there's this creative Word, present and active in the first creation, a *personal* Word who has entered human history, who "became flesh and lived among us." The obvious implication is that something unique is about to happen. A new creation is about to begin. The One at whose command all things came into existence enters the cosmos itself to begin a totally new chapter in human history.

Although there are many enormous differences between the gospels of Luke and John, they're in agreement on the one point mentioned earlier. We had nothing to do with the first Creation. We weren't there. But we're invited to play an active role in the second. The implied melancholy of the Word's having been rejected by "his own people" is at least partially diminished by his giving "power to become children of God" to those who *do* receive him. The new creation is still God's sovereign initiative and action, but participation in it appears to be voluntary. The machinery is all in place, but it doesn't seem to function until we make a conscious choice or decision. God has uttered the creative Word. But the power of that Word remains dormant in us until we acquiesce and, from the heart, say something like Mary's "Let it be with me according to your word" (Luke 1:38). The banquet is ready, and the invitations have been sent. What happens next is up to those who have been invited.

Has John set out consciously to write a second Genesis and tailored his material to fit that pattern? I don't believe so. Rather, it seems that as he internalized and reflected on what he knew about the life and ministry of Jesus, he saw a number of parallels, and a Genesis pattern naturally emerged. The facts determine the form and not vice versa.

The double nature of Jesus, the human and the divine, is nowhere better seen than in John's telling of the story. Sometimes we seem to see in Jesus the creative Word at work, while at other times the image is that of the Second Adam. Sometimes it is both.

Take, for example, the brief episode in which John describes the calling of the first disciples. Andrew, intrigued by his first encounter with Jesus, calls his brother Simon and brings him along. "Jesus…looked at him and said, 'You are Simon son of John. You are to be called Cephas' (which is translated Peter)" (John 1:42).

In the Garden of Eden, Adam was given the power to name the animals. Here the Second Adam begins to exercise his rightful dominion in this new creation by renaming Simon. In the old creation, Simon might have continued with his given trade of commercial fishing. In the new, that future is changed. The Gospels give us a graphic picture of the gradual transformation of this eager but stumbling disciple into a strong and fearless leader of the early Christian community. Peter, the Rock. Jesus, the Second Adam, gives Simon a new name. Jesus, the Creative Word, gives him a new future.

The classic name of God, YHWH (Exodus 3:14), is sometimes translated, "I am who I am," but it may just as easily be rendered, "I will be who I will be." The future tense appears to describe more accurately the God of the Bible, a dynamic God, God on the move, God who has the power to use the future tense and speak of what will be when the new creation is completed. In the Beatitudes, the future is applied to groups, "they will be comforted…they will be filled…they will be called children of God." Here it's specific—"'You are to be called Cephas' (which is translated Peter)."

Signs

When John speaks of what the other gospel writers call miracles, he selects seven to serve as his examples, perhaps thinking of the seven days of the

Creation account. And he calls them *signs* rather than miracles, signs that point to and reveal something beyond the events themselves.

The first sign is the changing of water into wine at a wedding feast in Cana of Galilee (see John 2:1-11). It's a remarkable story in many ways, and from one point of view, a strange way for Jesus to begin his ministry and "show his glory." Wouldn't a public healing be more appropriate? How does the manufacture of several hundred gallons of wine reveal God's glory? As a miracle it is indeed spectacular. However, when looked at as a sign, a deeper meaning emerges.

One of the major Old Testament metaphors of God's relationship with his people is that of marriage. God is the bridegroom and God's people the bride. "As the bridegroom rejoices over the bride, so shall your God rejoice over you," Isaiah records God as saying. The Sinai covenant, the Torah, is viewed as a marriage ceremony, and any transgression against that covenant was regarded as a form of adultery. Idolatry, oppression of orphans and widows, profaning the Sabbath—all were viewed as breaking the marriage commitment. A "sinful and adulterous generation" does not *necessarily* refer to people who have broken the seventh commandment.

John apparently sees this episode as God's initiative to heal the broken relationship and renew the marriage vows once more. The old is being replaced by the new. The water jars "for the Jewish rites of purification" symbolize the old ways of mending relationships between God and his people. Jesus' provision of wine for the feast seems to be linked to God's earlier promises of a new beginning on "that day," the day when God would come to act decisively on behalf of all his people. Among the prophetically described characteristics of this final intervention will be the swallowing up of death and the wiping away of tears from all people, and the day will be celebrated with a banquet and an abundance of wine. There will be "a feast of rich food, a feast of well-aged wines" (Isaiah 25:6).

When the host at a Middle Eastern wedding feast decided that the guests had been there long enough (usually several days), he could signal the end of the festivities by serving water to the guests instead of wine. It may well be that the servants interpreted Jesus' command to draw from the stone pots they had just filled up with water as the signal that the party was over. In reality, it was just beginning!

Water
Awakened one day
From the drowsy daily task
Of washing hands and feet,
At Cana heard
The long forgotten voice
Of One who calls with authority
And from scullery scrubbing
Found herself, Cinderella-like
Invited to the Feast
By the Guest turned Host.
Dressed in her brightest red
She pranced into the house
To delight and bewilder.

Other Signs

And what of the other miraculous events recorded by John? As miracles they reveal God's power, but as signs they appear to indicate that all of those things we've come to take for granted in the old creation—things such as disease, hunger, blindness, even death itself—will become *unnatural* in the new creation. As signs they point to that future so beautifully described in Revelation:

And I heard a loud voice from the throne saying,

"See, the home of God is among mortals.
He will dwell with them as their God;
they will be his peoples,
and God himself will be with them;
he will wipe every tear from their eyes.
Death will be no more;
mourning and crying and pain will be no more,
for the first things have passed away." (Revelation 21:3-4)

The new creation has been initiated but obviously not yet completed. There's always the tension between the already and the not yet. But in the meantime, there are signs of good things yet to come!

One of the signs, the healing of the paralytic at the pool of Beth-zatha (Bethesda), is the occasion for another clear reference to the new creation. Jesus did it on the Sabbath, and some of his enemies were quick to accuse him of Sabbath breaking. By way of reply, Jesus said, "My Father is still working, and I also am working" (John 5:17). After the first Creation, God rested, but in the new creation, the Sabbath has not yet come.

On one level, healing on the Sabbath might look like a clever device employed by Jesus to force his detractors to admit his power. In order to accuse him of Sabbath breaking, they would be forced to admit the miracle. But there's much more to it than that. In our Sabbath-starved society it's hard for us to appreciate the pivotal role the Sabbath played in Jewish thought and practice. Genesis tells us that "on the seventh day God finished the work that he had done, and he rested on the seventh day.... So God blessed the seventh day and hallowed it" (Genesis 2:2-3). Jesus said that the Sabbath was made for our sake—its observance is to be seen more as a welcome gift than as an onerous obligation. A modern Jewish theologian speaks of the observance of the seventh day as an example of "the sanctification of time" and says that "the Sabbaths are our great cathedrals; and our Holy of Holies is a shrine that neither the Romans nor the Germans were able to burn. The seventh day is...not a date but an atmosphere."3

For healing the man at the pool, Jesus was accused of violating this great institution. But in reality he was doing just the opposite. He was showing just how holy the Sabbath is, that it is indeed made for us and not we for it, and that in the new creation, unlike in the dictionary, "restoration" comes *before* "rest."

Born Again?

One of the clearest images of the new creation is found in the familiar story of Nicodemus, the prominent Pharisee who was fascinated by Jesus but felt it necessary to visit him by night, presumably to avoid being seen by other Pharisees. Sort of like a churchwarden sneaking into a triple-X-rated movie. We have only the barest summary of what must have been a lengthy conversation. (Middle Eastern custom would demand at least half an hour of small talk and mutual courtesies before getting around to the main subject.)

At the center of it all is Jesus' admonition to Nicodemus that he must be "born again" if he's to see or enter the kingdom of God. Scholars are fond of pointing out that the Greek word for *again* can also be translated as "from above." Either way, it refers back to John's prologue in which those who receive Jesus are given "power to become children of God." Whether "from above" or "again," it's a question of rebirth, of beginning again, of being re-created. It isn't a matter of adding a new dimension to the old life but of getting a brand-new life.

No wonder Nicodemus misunderstood. The notion is outlandish. How, indeed, can one be born again, re-created, made new? Jesus refused to give a direct answer. "How" questions can so easily deteriorate into matters of mere intellectual curiosity. This is far too important for that. Rather, he implied that only the Spirit of God can accomplish such a miracle. And a miracle it must be.

A story is told of a New England town meeting called to discuss the need for a new city hall. After much discussion, the town passed three resolutions: (1) We will build a new hall; (2) We'll build it using the materials from the old hall; and (3) Until the new one is built, we'll continue using the old one. The impossibility is obvious!

However, when we come to the matter of rebirth, we simply have no choice. We're compelled to do the impossible, to continue to use the old town hall while the new one is being built. We can't escape our bodies. This is why conversion is painful: We have to live in the house while it's being remodeled.

It's also why there's no such thing as instantaneous conversion. There may indeed be something that appears to be an instantaneous *beginning* of a conversion—such as Paul's encounter with the living Christ on the road to Damascus. But closer examination usually discloses that something has been fermenting under the surface for a long time before it emerges and becomes visible, and everyone, including Paul, would bear witness to the fact that the unfolding of what may have *begun* in a moment is a lifelong process. New creation is not a matter of simply rearranging the broken pieces of our former lives, but of permitting God to make something totally new.

Fortunately for us, this story doesn't end with this brief encounter. As if to illustrate the fact that the death of the old and the birth of the new takes time, John permits us to see Nicodemus move from the safety of his nocturnal anonymity to a moment where he puts his old values at some risk by becoming a tentative defender of Jesus (John 7:50-51), and finally to the point where he's willing to risk both his reputation and his livelihood by being publicly identified with Jesus (John 19:39). That's quite a journey.

Rebirth is not simply a change of religious parties, but a radical reordering of our whole understanding of life, the world, and our place in it. Not simply a new allegiance, like putting an "Under New Management" sign on the door when a large corporation swallows up a smaller one, while continuing to do the same old job.

Unfortunately, in our culture, being "born again" has often been trivialized by being equated with almost any intense religious experience or any emotion-laden encounter with the self or with God, however "God" might be defined. But when viewed through the Creation lens, it becomes synonymous with total conversion. One writer puts it this way: "There are no neutral zones or areas of life left untouched by biblical conversion. It is never solely confined to the inner self, religious consciousness, personal morality, intellectual belief, or political opinion. If we believe the Bible, every part of our lives belongs to the God who created us and intends to redeem us. No part of us stands apart from God's boundless love, no aspect of our life remains untouched by the conversion that is God's call and God's gift to us."[4]

The Tree of Life

The feeding of the five thousand is the only miracle story that shows up in all four gospel accounts, which I take to be a sign of its importance to all of the New Testament communities. In John's account, Jesus uses the occasion to speak of himself as the "bread of life." "Whoever eats of this bread will live forever; and the bread that I will give for the life of the world is my flesh," he says. Then he adds, "Unless you eat the flesh of the Son of Man and drink his blood, you have no life in you" (John 6:51,53). Such language stunned his hearers. To many it sounded like cannibalism, and worse, it reminded them of the Torah's strict prohibitions about the drinking of blood. What could he possibly mean? Apparently it was too much for some of them. They walked away and abandoned his cause.

Sacramentally minded commentators have assumed that this discourse about eating his flesh and drinking his blood was Jesus' way of anticipating what he would do on that fateful "night in which he was betrayed." The narrative makes it clear that although his apostles didn't join those who walked away, they probably didn't understand the words any better than anyone else. Perhaps it wasn't until that fateful supper took place and Jesus said, "This is my body...[and] this is my blood" that the light began to dawn and they could say to themselves, "Ah, *that* is what he meant back there in Capernaum."

With his Creation lens firmly in place, John sees—and hears—an additional dimension. Jesus is speaking about *life,* abundant life, the life of the age to come, eternal life, and he speaks of *himself* as its source. John remembers the Tree of Life in the first Creation story. God expelled the man and the woman from Eden to prevent their eating of this tree, apparently concerned that they might live forever in their now-damaged condition. The tree of life remained behind them, forever out of reach of human hands, a poignant memory of the way things might have been had other choices been made.

Now, John concludes, God has decided that in the new creation there must also be a Tree of Life, and connecting these strange words about eating Jesus' flesh and drinking his blood with subsequent events, he sees a remarkable image. God, he implies, will uproot the tree from Eden, and its wood will be used to fashion a cross that will be planted on a hill just outside the city of Jerusalem where all may have access to it. And the fruit on the tree will be nothing less than Jesus himself.

In his account of the Last Supper, you'll remember, John makes no reference to the taking and blessing of bread and wine. Rather, Jesus washes the disciples' feet. He audaciously improves on Moses by giving them a "new commandment"—that they love one another—and he illustrates by his own actions the inauguration of a new order in which power will be exercised in service to others.

In a sense, John has no need to describe the Eucharistic action, since the "breaking of bread" was already one of the distinguishing characteristics of the budding Christian community. At the heart of first-generation Christian worship, said a prominent liturgical scholar, was "a thing of absolute simplicity—the taking, blessing, breaking, and giving of bread, and the taking, blessing, and giving of a cup of wine and water, as these were first done with their new meaning by a young Jew before and after supper with his friends on the night before he died."[5]

What was this new meaning? It was, after all, a Passover meal, one of the holiest of all Jewish festivals, celebrated for centuries in remembrance of the Israelites' deliverance from Egyptian slavery. Moses and the children of Israel had been set free in order to be formed into a new nation. Bold enough to improve the Ten Commandments, Jesus seems to say that what he's about to do will provide a liberation even greater than the crossing of the Red Sea. "Do this in remembrance of *me*." Paul was not slow to pick up the reference when he wrote to the Corinthian church, "Christ our passover is sacrificed for us: therefore let us keep the feast" (1 Corinthians 5:7-8, KJV).

John doesn't isolate the meal from the Crucifixion that followed hard on its heels. The imagery is graphic. John can see Jesus as the Second Adam, nailed to a cross, and he seems to hear the voice of God whisper, "It is not good for this man to be alone." Jesus falls into the deep sleep, which we call death, and a soldier pierces his side with a spear. The parallels seem to multiply. No rib is taken from the wounded side; instead, water and blood pour forth. This fact is so important to John that he underlines it verbally: "He who saw this has testified so that you also may believe. His testimony is true, and he knows that he tells the truth" (John 19:35).

Water and blood are great biblical symbols. Water, the symbol of the Holy Spirit and of baptism. Blood, the symbol of sacrifice and sacrament. As Eve was born from the wounded side of the first Adam, so a second Eve—the bride of Christ, the church—is born from the wounded side of the Second Adam. Baptism speaks to us of Christian initiation, that mysterious interaction between God and human beings through which we somehow become members, living parts of a body of which Christ is the head. It gives birth to the bride, the Christian church. And Eucharist is the foretaste of the heavenly banquet, that food from the future, which nourishes the bride in her earthly pilgrimage.

Finishing the Work

Early in John's telling of the story, Jesus said, "My food is to do the will of him who sent me and to complete his work" (John 4:34). And as he prays the night before the crucifixion, Jesus tells the Father that he has glorified the Father's name by finishing the work he was sent to do (John 17:4). In the first part of the Creation story, we're told that on the seventh day, God *finished* the work that he had done. As Jesus comes to the end of his earthly ministry, the work of the new creation is being completed.

The chronology is fluid, but the thought is carried to its conclusion in Jesus' cry from the cross, "It is finished!" Far from being a word of defeat, it is heard as a shout of triumph. The first phase of the new creation is coming to an end. Jesus dies, having accomplished his task, and is given a hasty burial because the Sabbath is about to begin. And his tomb is in a garden.

The Bible tells of two axial events, two events that changed forever the historical landscape and gave a new identity to large groups of people. The first was the Exodus from Egypt, and the second was the resurrection of Jesus. The Exodus is the formative moment in the history of the Jewish people even as the Resurrection is in the history of Christians. It's worth noting that both happened when the human actors were powerless to do anything. As the people of God saw the Red Sea before them and the Egyptian armored divisions pursuing them from the rear, Moses said, "All you have to do is to stand still and see the glory of the Lord." And the small band of Jesus' faithful followers were powerless even to finish the funeral for their Master because of the inactivity required by the Sabbath.

As a result, both Jews and Christians are forced to confess that their greatest victories were not *won* but *given,* that they owe their existence to God and not to any great hero or heroine of the faith. Moses did not divide the Red Sea, and it was certainly not the faith of the apostles that raised Jesus from the dead. Both were acts of new creation.

The First Day

The gospel accounts are in agreement that what happened next happened on the first day of the week. That's creation day, the day on which God first said, "Let there be light!" If that were not enough, it all happened in a garden, a detail that immediately turns our minds back to the Genesis Creation story in which God and his new creatures, Adam and Eve, met face to face in a garden. John tells the story of Mary Magdalene's encounter with the risen Jesus whom she mistakes for the *gardener.* It has all the flavor of a story that Mary must have told on herself over and over again, even to the point of preserving her Aramaic form of address, *Rabboni,* when she finally recognizes him. ("Oy veh!" I can hear her saying. "I thought he was the *gardener!*")

Finally, John describes the first encounter between this resurrected Jesus and his small band of followers. The disciples were huddled together behind locked doors for fear that what had happened to Jesus might happen to them. In a sense, that was exactly what was about to occur, but not as they imagined.

Jesus appeared in their midst and gave the familiar greeting, "Shalom!" "Peace be with you." Then, apparently to reassure them that they were not hallucinating, he showed them his wounded hands and side. In an understatement that sounds more British than Jewish, John continues, "Then the disciples were glad when they saw the Lord." Glad? They must have been ecstatic! Some may have remembered the words of a familiar Passover psalm, the 126th, which begins, "When the LORD restored the fortunes of Zion, we were like those who dream. Then our mouth was filled with laughter, and our tongue with shouts of joy." Apparently the celebration was so boisterous that Jesus had to repeat his greeting, perhaps this time with a finger to his lips, "Peace!"

And then, with a message and a gesture that made them active participants rather than passive spectators in this new act of creation, he said to them, "As the Father has sent me, even so I send you." Then, as God had done with his mudman in Eden, he breathed on them and said, "Receive the Holy Spirit." A small band of emerging Adams and Eves is commissioned to continue the work.

While the accounts of the Resurrection appearances differ in some of their details, much as we would expect to happen when different witnesses bring their own memories to the table, they're agreed on one point. The One who walked out of the tomb had somehow been transformed, not simply resuscitated. It was as though in the darkness of the tomb, God had once again spoken the divine fiat, "Let there be light," and one form of matter—a dead body—had perhaps been transformed into energy, and that energy into a new form of matter—something never before seen, a resurrected human being. Both Paul and John describe Jesus as "the firstborn from the dead" (Colossians 1:18; see also Revelation 1:5). Elsewhere Paul called him, "the firstborn within a large family." His is the first Resurrection in the new creation, but the promise is that there will be many more. "Just as we have borne the image of the man of dust, we will also bear the image of the man of heaven" (1 Corinthians 15:49).

I want to see a new translation of the Bible into the hearts and conduct of living men and women. I want an improved translation—or transference it might be called—of the commandments and promises and teachings and influences of this Book to the minds and feelings and words and activities of the men and women who hold on to it and swear by it.... It is of no use making correct translations of words, if we cannot get the words translated into life.

—GENERAL WILLIAM BOOTH,
FOUNDER OF THE SALVATION ARMY

Blessed be the God and Father of our Lord Jesus Christ! By his great mercy he has given us a new birth into a living hope through the resurrection of Jesus Christ from the dead.

—1 PETER 1:3

FOUR

THE CONSEQUENCES

YBH?

We ended the last chapter with an amazing promise. "Just as we have borne the image of the man of dust, we will also bear the image of the man of heaven." Such a promise raises a vital question.

An English friend once told me that the margins of his religious books were filled with the notation "YBH?" It stood for "Yes, but how?" He was impatient, he said, with religious writers who draw wonderful word pictures of the kingdom of God but offer no clues about how to turn the pictures into reality. It would be like a dentist extolling the virtues of good dental hygiene but failing to mention toothpaste and brushes and floss. They ignore what preachers call the "application." Few things could be more frustrating than to be handed a picture of an idyllic world or church where people love each other, forgive each other, act like Jesus toward one another, and then to be told simply, "Just do it!" *Yes, but how?*

What must happen in order for God's dreams to come true, for us to begin to "bear the image of the man of heaven"? What is the impact of the new creation? What are the practical implications of looking at the biblical story through the Creation lens? It is literally a change in our point of view. But what difference does it make? That's almost like asking what difference the resurrection of Jesus makes.

Resurrection and the Recovery of Hope

The first tangible sign that a new creation has begun is the resurrection of Jesus. He once said that there were some people standing near him who would not taste death before they saw the kingdom of God coming in power (Mark 9:1). The empty tomb stands as a silent yet thunderous witness to the fulfillment of that promise.

It's virtually impossible to overestimate either the importance or the centrality of the resurrection of Jesus. Simply put, the Christian faith stands or falls on the reality of that event. Likewise, our whole understanding of the new creation and the recovery of hope depends on its historicity. If Jesus was raised, then life—yours and mine—has a visible and knowable direction and purpose. If he wasn't, then all bets are off. Even the moral and ethical teaching of Jesus depends on the Resurrection for validation. So much of what Jesus said depended on his own authority—"You have heard it said (in the Torah)...but I say to you..." If his death were the end, he would simply join a long list of failed messiahs and messianic pretenders.

For Paul, there were no gray areas on this subject—it was either black or white, and he was brazenly unapologetic about it—"If Christ has not been raised, your faith is futile" (1 Corinthians 15:17). He even had a list of specific people to whom the risen Jesus had appeared (1 Corinthians 15:5-9). The modern novelist John Updike has captured some of this defiant confidence in his *Seven Stanzas at Easter:*

Make no mistake: if He rose at all
It was as His body;
If the cells' dissolution did not reverse, the molecules reknit, the
    amino acids rekindle
the Church will fall...

Let us not mock God with metaphor,

Analogy, sidestepping transcendence;

Making of the event a parable, a sign painted in the faded
     credulity of earlier ages:

Let us walk through the door.[1]

Some truths are so profound and far-reaching that they can only be communicated through the use of metaphor—"The Lord is my shepherd," "You are the light of the world," "I am the bread of life," "Your word is a lamp to my feet and a light to my path," "I am the vine and you are the branches"—the list could go on and on. But to reduce the Resurrection to a metaphor for any new beginning or for the coming of spring after the death of winter is to trivialize the gospel story and to mock the very heart of the Christian faith. The same must be said of attempts to "explain" it as something that happened *only* in the minds of the disciples as they came to a deeper appreciation of their dead leader. Such efforts succeed in preserving a Christian vocabulary, but only by emptying the words of their true meaning.

It would be metaphor, for example, to say that Martin Luther King Jr. lives on in the struggles for racial justice and equality. But that isn't the same thing as resurrection, and so far as I know, no one claims to have seen King alive after his burial. Resurrection is a solid reality, not simply a fond memory. Hope is an "anchor for the soul," says the letter to the Hebrews, but an anchor needs something more substantial to grasp than a figure of speech. A metaphorical resurrection will be of help only to those whose faith is metaphorical too.

However, the effects of the event were so cosmic that they can't be adequately described without the use of metaphor and simile. The apostles bore witness to the Resurrection, not as some isolated and bizarre event, such as might be headlined in the supermarket tabloids ("Dead Rabbi Seen Alive by Followers!"), but as something that transformed the very nature of all reality. They not only experienced it—they entered into it. Or, as someone put it, they "lived in it, as in a new country." Updike said, "Let us walk through the door." And in a wonderfully descriptive phrase, C. S. Lewis said, "All the leaves of the New Testament are rustling with the rumor that one day we shall get inside."

Prisoner of Hope

A personal anecdote might help illustrate what it's like to "get inside," what happens when you "walk through the door."

For me, Lent in 1972 was not just a liturgical season, part of the church year, but a time of personal spiritual pain and penitence as well. Several personal and family problems had led to a crisis of faith. Until the fall of the previous year, I had been serving as bishop of the Episcopal Church in Guatemala. Guatemala in those days was a country torn apart by an undeclared civil war involving military death squads on the political right and Marxist guerrilla groups on the left. My few modest public attempts to suggest some peaceful alternatives and an end to the organized assassinations angered the military government, and in late 1971 they denounced me as a "subversive agent" and expelled me and my family from the country.

They didn't give us much time to get organized and make arrangements for an orderly departure—just forty-eight hours—so the next two days were days of enormous upheaval. It isn't the kind of thing you make contingency plans for. The only flight that would get us out of the country in time to meet the deadline went to Miami, so we landed there. The Episcopal bishop in Miami kindly offered us temporary lodging, but we had no sense of security about where we would finally end up or what we would do.

The forced and immediate separation from the people we loved and among whom we had lived was a painful experience. I couldn't avoid the feeling that somehow I had let them down. But being so quickly uprooted forced me to face some other things that were going on, some unpleasant ambiguities in my own life.

On the outside, thanks to a few national news stories about the event, was the image of a brave cleric doing battle with the powers of darkness. The House of Bishops of the Episcopal Church commended me for my "courage and commitment to social justice." But the outer facade did not match the inner reality. I talked a lot about justice, but I had never been able to alter my lifestyle enough for it to reflect the values I proclaimed. I often preached about prayer but rarely prayed. I spoke warmly of so-called family values but neglected my own family in my pursuit of clerical success. As a result, my marriage was strained, two of our teenagers were involved in drug use, one of them so deeply that he was virtually a stranger under our roof. And I was in great danger of becoming chemically addicted to sleeping pills and alcohol.

Some temporary relief came when a friendly bishop offered me a job as student chaplain at the University of Arkansas, but we both knew it was not to be a permanent position. Our family's future was uncertain.

One morning while I was taking care of some paperwork at the student center, the phone rang. I recognized the voice as that of a member of a small prayer group that I had been asked to work with. In her heavy Arkansas drawl, she asked, "Bishop, do you believe in the resurrection of Jesus?"

My response was almost automatic. This was a simple theological inquiry for which I had a pat answer. "Why, of course," I said, "the Resurrection is the central doctrine of the Christian faith."

"That's not what I mean, Bishop. Do you believe in the resurrection of Jesus?"

I responded impatiently, "I just told you. The Resurrection is at the heart of all Christian belief. It's the keystone in the arch of faith, and all other Christian doctrines depend on it for support."

"You're still not hearing me, Bishop," my friend replied. "Do *you* believe in the resurrection of Jesus?"

By now I was getting exasperated, and this time I shouted into the phone, "Yes, by God, I *do* believe in the resurrection of Jesus!"

Her reaction was fascinating. "Far out!" she said. (People talked that way in the seventies.) "I didn't know bishops really believed that stuff. That's cool!"

My reaction was totally different. I had often prayed Paul's prayer, "I want to know Christ and the power of his resurrection" (Philippians 3:10). And as I shouted into the phone, I realized that the prayer had been answered. I *did* believe in the resurrection of Jesus, not simply as a matter of assent to the Bible's witness, but from the depths of my heart. It came as close to certainty as anything I had ever experienced and made what I had formerly called faith look like mere suspicion.

The result was what I can only describe as a supernaturalizing of my world. As I walked home for lunch that day, the sky seemed bluer, the leaves on the trees greener, the atmosphere almost electric, and my heart had been filled with an unexpected hope. It was as though I had stumbled into a new world, or as though the old one had been made new.

My situation was something like that of the first witnesses to the Resurrection. In one sense, nothing had changed, and yet everything was different. They still had to face the hostility of unbelievers and the persecution that followed. But they did so with an astounding joy and vitality and with an unquenchable hope. When death dies, all of its parasitic confederates—fear, anxiety, despair, and all that lot—lose their source of strength. My difficulties and problems had not disappeared, but they were drained of their dominion. The circumstances of my life were exactly as they had been earlier that morning, but their power to intimidate was gone. If God actually *had* raised Jesus from the dead, then my problems looked tiny by comparison. The resurrection of Jesus had become a door that opened into a new life. It was only later that I remembered what Paul had said, that the same power God used in raising Jesus from the dead is at work in those of us who believe (Ephesians 1:19-20).

The months that followed proved just how true that is. That power quickly began the process of setting both me and our children free from our addictions and began to weld our whole family together as never before. And I would have to say, thirty years later, that the creative force of the Resurrection has not been diminished in our lives.

I still observe Lent as an aid to devotion, as a vital part of the liturgical year. But my personal Lent ended that year. Since that time I have been a captive of the Resurrection, or, as the prophet Zechariah puts it, a prisoner of hope (9:12).

Making the Connections

Preachers face the daunting task of helping people make the connections between what they hear in a sermon and what they experience in their daily lives. John Stott described this enterprise as bridging the gap "between two worlds"—the world of biblical reality and the world of contemporary experience. Evangelical preachers, he said, frequently stick to the biblical side of the chasm, "shooting arrows straight up," while more liberal preachers do the same thing from the contemporary or experiential side, with neither group reaching across the divide and making the necessary connections.

Though it's usually overlooked in descriptions of the Resurrection, one of the first things the risen Jesus did was to conduct a Bible study, presumably to enable his followers to bridge the gap between the two worlds. Luke describes his doing this twice. The first time was with two downhearted disciples who were walking to Emmaus on that first Easter day. "Beginning with Moses and all the prophets, he interpreted to them the things about himself in all the scriptures" (Luke 24:27). And the effect was electrifying: "Were not our hearts burning within us…while he was opening the scriptures to us?" (verse 32).

The second time was apparently a bit later on the same day when Jesus appeared to the "eleven and their companions." Once again he "opened their minds to understand the scriptures."

Just which scriptures he might have explained is the subject of much speculation among scholars. Front-runners include Genesis 3:15; Deuteronomy 18:15; parts of Psalms 2, 16, 22, 110, and 118; Isaiah 7:14; 9:2-7, and chapters 52 and 53; Jeremiah 31:31-34; and Daniel 7:13-14.

Whatever the passages may have been, the fact that he explained them at all was typical of his kindness. We're accustomed to thinking of the *joy* of his followers on the first Easter day as they were encountered by the risen Christ, but what about their *bewilderment?* You don't expect the person you've buried on a Friday to drop in for a chat the following Sunday. They hadn't spent the Sabbath after the Crucifixion waiting expectantly for the Resurrection; they had spent it in grief and despair. He was dead, and as far as they knew, that was that. Their hopes had been utterly shattered. The women who went to the tomb were not expecting to find a risen Jesus. They were on their way to put the finishing touches on his burial, totally unaware that in reality they were on their way to the world's greatest surprise party.

What a mind-shattering experience it must have been when the world of their expectations and experience collided with the world of supernatural reality, when this world and the one to come suddenly overlapped and merged with each other! It was indeed "too good *not* to be true," but what in the world was going on? Resurrection demands an explanation. Jesus gave his followers a precious gift as he explained the biblical story.

You'll remember that Jesus had chastised the Sadducees for knowing "neither the Scriptures nor the power of God." Here, on the day of his resurrection, he had a chance to illustrate both things. By opening the Scriptures to his little band of confused followers, he revealed the power of God and enabled them to make the all-important connections between what they had known in the past and what was happening to them now.

It's a dangerous thing to interpret our personal experience without reference to God's revelation. A scientist would remind us that while getting the correct data is important, the correct *interpretation* of the data is essential. Apart from the biblical witness, any manifestation of God's power will invariably be misinterpreted. After Jesus' conflicts with the Jewish authorities, the disciples could easily have seen his resurrection as a complete break with the past, as God's having turned his back on the chosen people, and as the inauguration of an independent movement of faith.

Their Bible study led them to just the opposite conclusion. The Resurrection wasn't something that happened in isolation from the sacred memory of the Jewish people. It was connected. It wasn't merely consistent with the Scriptures. It was the Scriptures' clearest fulfillment.

A Fresh Image

This explanation not only made the connections, it made some radical changes, too. One of the first things to be changed was the disciples' image of God, or to be more precise, their image of what God was doing in Jesus. And that changed their image of Jesus, which in turn changed their image of themselves. Seeing Jesus' life in a new light gave them a new self-understanding. Today, after centuries of reflection and experience, we can speak confidently about the two natures of Jesus, the human and the divine. But except for one brief moment on a mountaintop, in the presence of Peter and James and John, Jesus' divinity was hidden beneath his skin. It wasn't visible to others.

The Messiah expected by pious first-century Jews was a purely human one, and up through the events of Good Friday, Jesus could be looked at in those terms. Like other rabbis of his day, he had gathered a school of disciples. He had taught them and encouraged them to share his teaching with others. While the miraculous events, the "signs" as John called them, set him apart from other teachers, the effect of the miracles was still somewhat limited.

Jesus may have been thought of as an exceptional human being, but a human being nonetheless. He could be viewed as a moral teacher or prophet who was endowed with certain miraculous powers. He was a gifted rabbi. And there was certainly nothing unusual in the matter of his death. Crucified prisoners suffered terribly—then they died. Just as Jesus did.

But the Resurrection opened a new dimension. Paul was thinking about this transformation when he wrote, "From now on, therefore, we regard no one from a human point of view; even though we once knew Christ from a human point of view, we know him no longer in that way. So if anyone is in Christ, there is a new creation: everything old has passed away; see, everything has become new!" (2 Corinthians 5:16-17).

Everything! From this new point of view, everything looks different. We get new insight into the activity of God, what he is doing and what he is willing to do. And as Paul says, "we regard no one from a human point of view." Christians can no longer look at other people and simply see finite human beings. "Life is hard, then you die," says the bumper sticker. The Resurrection says that's only half the story. "You have never met a mere mortal," wrote C. S. Lewis. New creation means new life.

No Graven Images

And new life means that our relationship with God is a dynamic and ever-expanding experience. Hence, our image of God will undergo a number of periodic overhauls. All of us have some sort of image of God. It may not be a pictorial image, but at the very least it involves some kind of assessment of who he is, and what he might or might not do. Whether this image or vision is the product of years of extensive rational reflection or simply the sum of our conscious and unconscious responses to the Divine, it is, for each of us, a sacred space, often very private and very personal. As a result, we become protective of it and are immediately suspicious of anyone or anything that threatens to change it.

But change it must. There are two major dangers associated with an image of God. The first is confusing it with the reality it's meant to represent. God is God; our images are not. God is infinite; our images are limited by the narrowness of our own comprehension.

The second danger is that an image can become an idol. The second commandment warns us against making "graven images." Our Jewish forbears took this word seriously. The story is told of the Romans who sacked Jerusalem in A.D. 70 going into the temple's Holy of Holies, eager to see an image of the Jewish god, only to find an empty room. (Parenthetically it might be said that for the women who went to finish the funeral for Jesus, his tomb would have been a holy place. But it, too, was empty.) The prohibition was originally a warning about confusing a creature with the Creator, against kneeling at the altar of our own imaginations, against worshiping the works of our hands instead of the God who gave us hands in the first place. But this "second word" has another, often overlooked, aspect to it. It has to do not so much with what idols are made of, but with their changelessness. They are static not active. They always remain the same. The only change a graven image can undergo is decoration or decay. We can decorate them, clothe them with fancy garments, much as some statues of saints are adorned. Or exposed to the elements—the eroding influence of sun, wind, and rain, or the toxic myths that permeate our culture—they'll deteriorate. The one thing a graven image cannot do is *grow.*

In *Prince Caspian,* one of C. S. Lewis's *Chronicles of Narnia,* a young girl, Lucy, meets the Christ-figure, Aslan, after a long absence:

"Aslan," said Lucy, "you're bigger."

"That is because you are older, little one," answered he.

"Not because you are?"

"I am not. But every year you grow, you will find me bigger."[2]

Lewis says that at this point Lucy was so happy she didn't want to speak. I can understand why. "Be still and know that I am God," wrote the psalmist, and T. S. Eliot said that "in the mystical encounter with the Divine, power over language is lost."

In every relationship we have, the mental image of the other person is constantly growing. The more time we spend with another person, the better we get to know them; the better we get to know them, the better our assessment is of who they are. So it is with our relationship with the living God and, consequently, with our image of God. The more we mature, the more it grows. And the only alternative to growth is decay. Hence the need for periodic overhauls.

The first followers of Jesus must have gone through such overhauls on a regular basis. Their image of Jesus was one thing when he called them, another when they watched him heal the sick, yet another when he stilled the storm that threatened their little boat. Their understanding grew when he raised Lazarus from the dead but suffered grave damage when they saw him on the cross. They thought of him one way on Good Friday, but in a totally different way on Easter.

Rising Expectations

The mechanism that alters our image of God is a change in our expectations. Very often we see what we expect to see. And if our image of God is that of a distant moralist or an interested but uninvolved First Cause, we won't see a great deal. Worse, we'll be perpetual skeptics about any claim that God may have acted personally in human affairs, whether in healing our neighbor's child, or in raising Jesus from the dead. It will be hard for us to believe that God could really care about what happens to us. We'll be like those scholars who, assuming the impossibility of the miraculous, encourage us to search for the tiny fragments of history that may lie behind the biblical tales of divine intervention. Our expectations need to be raised.

In the months preceding my family's expulsion from Guatemala, in an attempt to make up for lost time in teaching the gospel to my children, I instituted a suppertime Bible study. No parent will be surprised to learn that my edict did not receive universal approval. There was palpable resistance, notably from the teenagers in the crowd—a lot of fidgeting in the chairs and periodic moans of "Is it over yet? Can we go now?" But I was undaunted and plowed ahead. I selected the gospel according to Mark, since it's the shortest of the four and I thought I had a pretty good chance of getting through it before Easter.

To this day, I don't know what effect, if any, the study had on my children, but I know that I experienced a personal revelation that resulted in a personal revolution. Chapter 6 of Mark's gospel begins with the story of Jesus returning to his hometown of Nazareth where he, too, met with some degree of resistance. It sounded familiar, just like what I was getting from my own children, and I took heart in Jesus' words that, "Prophets are not without honor, except in their hometown, and among their own kin, and *in their own house.*"

But my self-congratulatory musings were interrupted when the next verse jumped off the page and hit me between the eyes. Mark tells us that Jesus "could do no deed of power there [pause], except that he laid his hands on a few sick people and cured them." I had always thought that healing sick people was about as powerful as it gets, and here Mark virtually dismisses that as nothing in comparison to what Jesus might have done. He expected much more. I immediately realized that Mark's expectations and mine were light-years apart. Healing seemed pretty powerful to me. Now I was convinced that I expected too little from God. I needed what sociologists call a "revolution of rising expectations."

A revolution of rising expectations is what happens when people who are poor but unaware of their poverty, because they have only other poor people to compare themselves with, suddenly discover that not everyone is poor. They then begin to exert upward pressure on the power structures, demanding a greater share of the wealth. Such revolutions may be peaceful or they may be violent, but they usually effect some degree of change. But how in the world does this work when the poverty is spiritual poverty? And how do you exert upward pressure when the power structure is God? It boils down to a matter of prayer.

A New Way of Praying

Spiritual poverty isn't such a bad thing, biblically speaking, if you define it properly and know what to do about it. In fact, Jesus said that the poor in spirit were especially blessed or happy because the kingdom of heaven is theirs. One modern translation says, "How blest are those who know their need of God" (Matthew 5:3, NEB). In other words, spiritual poverty isn't meant to be a permanent state; it's meant to lead us to something far greater.

A number of years ago, at the end of an informal Eucharistic celebration in our cathedral in Denver, a woman came to me in tears. "These people," she said, "they seem to know God personally. I don't think I can go on much longer without some sign that the Holy Spirit is working in my life!" I said, "You have the sign already." She wiped her eyes and said, "What do you mean? What sign?" And I replied, "This need that you feel inside, this yearning for God. That's the sign. It's the Holy Spirit filling you with a hunger for the one thing that will make you whole. Your spiritual poverty is not a threat—it's a promise." And before the evening was over, she experienced a wondrous fulfillment of her deepest desire.

A remarkable Benedictine nun, reflecting on this strange kingdom paradox of the richness of poverty, wrote:

> Being poor in spirit means
> Having nothing to call your own
> Except your poverty
> It is a joyful awareness of your emptiness
> It is the soil of opportunity
> For God has space to work
> In emptiness that is owned.[3]

Years ago I heard Meredith Willson, the musician who wrote *The Music Man*, telling of a dream he had. In the dream he was one of many musicians playing before a great and wealthy king. The king was so impressed with the music that at the end of the concert he said, "Come, musicians, and fill your instruments with golden coins from my treasury."

Willson concluded, somewhat mournfully, "There I stood with my piccolo." If there's a moral to the tale, it is certainly that the one who brings the greatest emptiness to God takes away the greatest treasure.

When we realize our poverty and determine to do something about it, the revolution begins. And it begins with prayer. Not simply a prayer before undertaking a particular action. Prayer *is* the action. If I wanted to see the mighty works that Mark spoke of, if I wanted to see the kingdom of God at work, bringing about some new creation, I apparently had to change the way I prayed.

We Anglicans have been taught to pray politely and somewhat tentatively, like proper English ladies and gentlemen. We rely on the force of the words themselves to make our point and are embarrassed by shouted prayers or any other display of emotion. But I came to the conclusion that our self-imposed diffidence has little to do with biblical praying. Poverty of spirit, like any other poverty, can breed a sense of desperation. So I began to pray in a more urgent fashion, in a more expectant fashion, to "exert upward pressure on the power structure" and to "demand" a bigger piece of the spiritual pie. In today's language, I had to get in God's face.

While this sounds presumptuous, I was encouraged by remembering how Jesus told his disciples "to pray always and not to lose heart" and then told them that wonderfully humorous story about a widow who pestered the life out of a cold-hearted judge until he gave her what she wanted (Luke 18:1-8). And I remembered that Isaiah had given much the same advice: "You who remind the LORD, take no rest, and *give him no rest*" (Isaiah 62:6-7). After all, it isn't a matter of pressuring the Lord for what we want, but for what God has promised to give. Like the plaintive cry of a child to a parent, "But you promised!"

The immediate results of my new venture of prayer were disappointing. In fact, the only thing that I was aware of was an increasing sense of distance between my own spiritual dryness and what the New Testament seemed to describe as normal Christian experience. Where was the joy, the awareness of Christ's presence, the sure guidance of the Holy Spirit? If anything, the more I prayed, the more intense my desperation became.

It wasn't long after that we were expelled from Guatemala. To make matters worse, the government launched a propaganda campaign denouncing me and my ministry. I was falsely accused of being a Marxist, a political meddler, and a subversive agent of some unnamed conspiracy seeking to overthrow the government. One of my friends, a prominent Roman Catholic bishop, joined in the denunciation and was quoted as saying that he had long suspected that I was a communist.

Although I didn't make the connection at the time, it was at this moment that my prayers began to be answered. The accusations hurt, and even worse was the fact that some of our friends believed the propaganda. The forced separation from people we had come to know and love was extremely painful. But at the same time, I felt myself engulfed by a tangible and overwhelming feeling of peace, even a sense that what looked like a personal defeat might somehow be God's victory. I found that I had no hatred or hostility toward those responsible for our expulsion. I felt great compassion for my bishop friend, assuming that his denunciation was the result of some political pressure and threats.

Such emotions toward those who frustrate my plans and accuse me falsely have never come naturally to me. Quite the opposite, in fact. I knew that I had not manufactured them, and that they must be something God had created, that the Holy Spirit was somehow overruling my natural inclinations. This was my first inkling of the power of the new creation. I had known, of course, that Jesus had proclaimed blessings for those who are persecuted for the sake of justice, but I had always assumed that they were reserved for some heavenly future. Here they were happening in the here and now, and I was surprised and excited. The death of one thing, in this case my hopes and dreams about my future ministry, enabled the birth of something altogether different.

The new creation assumes that our old life is beyond repair or improvement. If we're to bear the image of the Man of heaven, the old life must die.

YBH? (Yes, but how?) In the following chapters, we'll examine the Three Things That Didn't Work—the Ark, the Law, and the Sword—and see how their images are fulfilled and redeemed in the new creation.

God has given us five things for the journey: water, bread, wine, a book, and each other.

—ATTRIBUTION UNKNOWN

God waited patiently in the days of Noah, during the building of the ark, in which a few, that is, eight persons, were saved through water. And baptism, which this prefigured, now saves you.

—1 PETER 3:20-21

In fulfillment of his own purpose he gave us birth by the word of truth, so that we would become a kind of first fruits of his creatures.

—JAMES 1:18

The Church's one foundation is Jesus Christ her Lord; she is his new creation, by water and the word.

—SAMUEL JOHN STONE

FIVE

THE NEW ARK

First Fruits

When our five children were younger, I used to wonder how I could best convince them of their father's love. I thought of many schemes and concocted several fantasies. In one, I imagined that I would parade all of them into the living room, seat myself in a large chair in the center, and say something like, "Now, children, listen very carefully, because I'm only going to say this once. Your father loves you very, very much. Now go, but whenever you find yourself in any distress, remember what I said and you will be comforted."

Obviously that was not satisfactory, so I devised another scheme. I would write each one of them a letter saying, "Dear Paul, Mark, Matthew, Peter, or Suzanna, your father loves you very much. Please carry this with you at all times, and whenever you need comfort or strength, take it out and read it, and you'll be helped. Love, Daddy."

Perhaps a minor improvement, but still not effective. Why? Because it still lacked the essential ingredient of personal presence and human touch. When children come running into the house crying because of a scraped knee or a battered ego, a memory, however vivid, and words, however well intentioned, are inadequate. They need the warmth of a human embrace. How many of us, attempting to minister God's love to confused or grieving people, have discovered, or rediscovered, this truth. Presence, not platitudes, is what brings comfort and healing.

I don't want to minimize the importance of memories and words. We're literally speechless without them. Without them we have no way to communicate with one another or to understand our world. But memories and words need family for their satisfactory completion. Memories grow more powerful when they are shared, and words need a place to become flesh before they can work their fullest healing power. It's simply not enough to post some information on a Web page. We are not disembodied spirits floating around in the ether. We have bodies, and bodies need to interact with other bodies. That may be why a new family is the first product of the new creation. Birth never takes place in a vacuum. Birth presupposes a family. The same is true for the new birth.

Making family and building community with otherwise unrelated people seem to have come naturally to Jesus. Mark tells us that he called his disciples "to be with him." He expanded his family when his mother and his brothers tried to interrupt him one day while he was teaching. Looking around at the crowd, he said that whoever does the will of his heavenly Father is his brother and sister and mother. He made a new family even while on the cross, commending Mary to the care of his disciple John, and John to Mary. And to the repentant thief he said, "Today, you will be *with me* in para-dise." So it should come as no surprise that the new creation brings a new community. Just as the Genesis account begins with a family, so this second creation story describes a new family. The God who "gives life to the dead and *calls into existence the things that do not exist*" (Romans 4:17) is at it again.

The first evidence of the power of the Resurrection is the creation of a new family. And this new family plays a major role in the biblical story. As it was in the beginning, is now, and ever shall be—it is not good for the man, or the woman, to be alone.

Parenthetically, it needs to be said that what we find in these biblical stories is not so much an endorsement of "family values" as an affirmation of the value of family. And even more challenging is the clear message that the natural family is not enough. In some cases it may even impede our participation in the new family, which is composed of all those who respond to Jesus' invitation.

Redefining the Symbols

In the new creation, there's new life for the old images. The metaphors of Ark, Law, and Sword will take on new meanings. The symbols of our failure have become signs of hope and expectation.

The last chapter ended with a question. Yes, but how? How do we gain access to the promised new life, and how do we experience the power of the Resurrection in our own lives? That, after all, is the key question. Here, perhaps, we need to phrase it differently. It should be "YBW?"—Yes, but *where?* Any authentic recovery of hope will take place in community with other people. Martin Buber, the great Jewish philosopher, understood this when he wrote, "We are waiting for a theophany (a visible manifestation of God's presence and glory) about which we know only its location, and that location is community."

The New Testament word for *community* is *koinonia.* It means "a deep sharing of life marked by the power and presence of the Holy Spirit." Paul referred to it in his familiar blessing, "The grace of the Lord Jesus Christ, and the love of God, and the [*koinonia* (sometimes translated 'fellowship' or 'communion')] of the Holy Ghost, be with you all" (2 Corinthians 13:14, KJV).

To speak of community is to speak of the church, and—fair warning—this may be where we'll see the starkest contrast between what is and what might be. There is, unfortunately, a great gulf fixed between what most of us experience in our regular church life and what we might experience were the Christian community to embrace the full implications of the new creation. However, a deeper awareness of just what the church is *designed* to be is the prerequisite for enabling it to become what it really is.

Viewed through our Creation lens, the biblical story says some exciting things about the nature and purpose of this new community, as well as its potential for transforming lives and offering fresh hope for the future. A fresh awareness of the tremendous potential that true Christian community offers is the first step toward the realization of that potential. In this chapter I want to explore what the story says and then offer some personal evidence to corroborate the biblical claims.

The Amazing Expanding Ark

The Christian community is the new Ark. In a great deal of Christian art, Noah's Ark is used as a symbol for the church. It's seen as the "Ark of salvation," the means of rescuing those who are being overwhelmed by the storms of life. But the very use of the image underscores the major differences between the old Ark and the new.

The old Ark was big—three hundred by fifty by thirty cubits, about the length of a football field and a half—but it couldn't get any bigger. And it had a specific but limited purpose—to save lots of animals plus eight people. In human terms it was primarily a refuge for the righteous few, the holy huddle.

The new Ark, on the other hand, is elastic, constantly expanding as more and more folk come aboard. If the other animals appear to be ignored, it's because the flood from which we need rescuing this time is sin, something that apparently only the human animal is capable of committing. As Mark Twain put it, "Man is the only animal that blushes. Or needs to."

The mission of this Ark is different too. The old Ark was a lifeboat, keeping its occupants safe until the flood disappeared. Its passenger list was limited. This Ark's purpose is to launch out into the deep, to ply the waters day and night searching for those who are being swept away by the flood, and to bring them to safety. Its passenger list is wide open. And, if I may stretch the metaphor a bit, those who do come aboard will be treated as welcome guests for a spell while they dry off and catch their breath. They'll be given clean clothes and invited to dine at the Captain's Table. But before long it will be pointed out that their new clothes are not leisure attire but uniforms; they aren't just passengers, but members of the crew. And they'll also discover that this Ark isn't a cruise ship, but a fishing boat.

To enter the new creation is to enter the realm in which God is active and working to remold the universe, beginning with his conscious collaborators, those who have yielded their allegiance to him.

The Preview of Coming Attractions

The story tells us that the good news—the gospel—is both information and invitation. The information is that, through the life, death, and resurrection of Jesus, the promises God made to the people of Israel in centuries past have begun to be fulfilled. The invitation is to join the new community created by these events, a community where the new creation is taking place—where the sins of the past can be forgiven and the transforming power of the Spirit is at work.

This community, or family, turns out to be more than an instrument for getting something done, like proclaiming the good news. It is that, of course, but it's also one of the elements of the good news. The new family is more than a means of communicating the gospel promises. In a deep sense, it's an integral part of the promises themselves. To put it another way, it's meant to be a body of people who can appropriate to themselves the very words of Jesus, "Come unto [us], all ye that labour and are heavy laden."

A contemporary theologian put it like this: "A baptized person is a sign of promise for all people. The Eucharist is a promise for every meal. The church is a promise for all human society." As another theologian put it (they often speak this way), it's the *"prolepsis of the eschaton,"* or, as they say at the movies, "the preview of coming attractions." Again, as we've seen in the other cases where we used the Creation lens to view the biblical story, the future becomes a major element in our vision. And this means that, though the church is rooted and grounded in historical reality, we can measure its faithfulness as much by seeing how closely it resembles the *future* as by how well it replicates the past. The question to ask of the church is this: Is this a community where the promises are being fulfilled, or is it merely a place where they're being discussed and debated?

The biblical word for *church* is *ecclesia*. Its root definition is something like "those who have been called, or called out." It's a gathering of God's chosen people, and surprising to our modern ears, the word carries absolutely no reference to buildings. As it's been said, the church is what's left after the building burns down. One denomination of American Pentecostal Christians was simply giving the word *ecclesia* a modern translation when they named themselves the "Assemblies of God." For hundreds of years the church's meetings were held in private homes. In our day and age, at least in Western society, so-called house churches are a novelty, but for the first two or three centuries that's all there was.

Beyond Individualism

Our modern tendency to think of ourselves as independent individuals makes it difficult to understand much of the biblical story. It's helpful to remember that every line in the Bible was penned by someone for whom nation, tribe, clan, and family were primary. Individual identity sprang from membership in a community. Where we—consciously or unconsciously—assume the truth of René Descartes's maxim, "I think, therefore I am," biblical writers would be more likely to say, "We are, therefore I am."

For example, in the parable of the prodigal son, the son's leaving home is taken as a tragedy. He's leaving his primary community. In our culture, we're usually relieved when an offspring strikes out on her own, and if we throw any parties, it's generally when the kid leaves, not when he or she comes back to roost. Or take the case of Zacchaeus, that reformed tax collector of Jericho, to whose house Jesus invited himself for lunch. When he announced that he was giving away half of his possessions to the poor, Jesus' response was, "Today salvation has come to *this house*" (Luke 19:9).

With the exception of the southern "You all" or "y'all," modern English lacks a plural pronoun for "you." As a result, we're in danger of misinterpreting a number of key New Testament passages where the word *you* appears. Most of the time, they're plural, not singular, and carry the assumption that God's people will be acting together as a visible community. "You are the salt of the earth," "You are the light of the world," "May you grow to the measure of the stature of the fullness of Christ."

Laboring under the many dangers and restrictions of the Nazi regime, Dietrich Bonhoeffer had a deep appreciation of the blessing of Christian community. He wrote,

Between the death of Christ and the last day it is only by a gracious
anticipation of the last things that Christians are privileged to live in
visible fellowship with other Christians. It is by the grace of God
that a congregation is permitted to gather visibly in this world to
share God's Word and sacrament.[1]

But Bonhoeffer would have been the first to recognize that this great
privilege is not simply given for the benefit of the saved. It's designed to
bless others. Biblically speaking, we're always blessed in order to be a blessing. William Temple, the archbishop of Canterbury during World War II,
encapsulated this truth in his observation that "the Church is the only
organization that exists primarily for the sake of those who are not its members." The greatest gift that this new community can give to a lost and
dying world is neither a list of instructions nor a bunch of moral maxims.
The greatest gift it can give is itself.

If a picture is worth a thousand words, we might say that a working
model is worth a thousand pictures. When the church, empowered by the
Spirit, and encouraged by the vision of the new creation, begins to resemble
something of the new life promised in the gospel, it offers a powerful anti-
dote to the cynicism that infects so much of society, and it becomes indeed
a preview of coming attractions. There can be no recovery of hope without
some tangible evidence that hope itself is justified, and that it is based on
solid experience and not wishful thinking. Imperfect as we are, we will be
modest in our claims and quick to acknowledge that the good in our common life is not so much the result of our own virtue, but the product of
God's life-giving Spirit.

But modesty does not require silence, and the very fact that there exists
a community in which one can find people whose priorities are being
formed by the gospel is good news. The fact that there are places where forgiveness and reconciliation are practiced, where broken relationships and

broken bodies are being healed, where all are welcomed and where there's tangible evidence of God's power to forgive sin and to set people free from its tyranny, is palpable evidence of the reality of new creation. Oh, it's far from complete. God isn't finished with us yet! But it is present, even in its imperfect and fragmentary form.

Life on Board

The Christian church proclaims good news, not good advice, and the good news must be visible in a living community. Educators tell us that people learn best when they're immersed in a community that models the teaching. A friend of mine who was both a prominent nuclear physicist and an Episcopal priest remarked that he became a Christian the same way he became a physicist. He didn't become a scientist, he said, simply by absorbing technical information, but by living with other scientists, watching what they did and learning from their activities—by becoming part of the scientific community.

We learn best by seeing the thing we need to learn being acted out by others. It's one thing to tell people that they should forgive their enemies, that they should be concerned about the marginalized and the outcasts, that they should speak the truth in love, and bear one another's burdens. It's another thing altogether to create communities where these things happen on a daily basis, where they're modeled and performed.

The new family is designed to be the kind of fellowship in which we can learn by doing, and thus become a microcosm of good things yet to come, a fragment of the future that has washed up on the doorstep of today. "See how those Christians love one another" was said of an earlier generation, and that example generated among outsiders a deep desire to belong to such a fellowship.

We are not designed to make the Christian journey alone. We're made for each other. Frodo Baggins wouldn't dare leave the Shire without the company of faithful companions. There are too many "dangers, toils, and snares" out there on the highway for anyone to venture out alone.

This is particularly true when we view the journey through the Creation lens. By nature, we seem to be more comfortable with the past than with the future. The biblical account of the Exodus gives us a graphic picture of this tendency. Whenever the going got tough, the people began to long for the old days and talk about returning to their captivity in Egypt. That, at least, was familiar and predictable. It's almost impossible to remain faithful to the new creation without a lot of encouragement from people who share the same vision. Without others at our side, we're very likely to feel like naive and isolated utopians attempting the impossible and to be tempted to give up the whole enterprise. I often think the one thing we humans fear more than slavery is freedom. Our old chains may have been uncomfortable, but at least they gave a sense of stability.

The Gangplank

If there's anything clear about the concept of new creation, it's that God's action in Jesus wasn't meant simply to modify our human condition, but to transform it by offering us a fresh beginning. We aren't called to be improved ("the new improved you!"), nor simply to have some fresh religious dimension added to our otherwise secular existence. We're called to die in order that we might be remade. The Potter must smash the imperfect vessel and begin again with the unformed clay. The old life, as the story implies, must give way to the new. The death and resurrection of Jesus has inaugurated a new creation. He has pioneered the way. Followers of Jesus are offered the opportunity to participate in this kingdom reality and to live in the power of the Resurrection.

But you may have noticed a problem with this concept. In order to be resurrected, Jesus had to die. He "was crucified, died, and was buried." Where does that leave us? If participation in what God is doing is dependent on our death, there will be few takers. Churches that require crucifixion for membership will be small. Few of us have a deep longing, much less a natural talent, for martyrdom.

Oscar Wilde said that to fall in love with oneself is to enter into a life-long romance. The greatest obstacle to our consenting to new birth lies precisely here. We've fallen in love with ourselves, miserable though we might be. Our personality, our ways of relating to life, the inflated mental image we have of ourselves, those little things that make us "us," all of these feel threatened with annihilation by the notion of rebirth. Who will I be on the other side? we ask. Will I still be me? If I lose my old life, what will I find to take its place? Those who have taken the plunge will tell you that the answer is "too good not to be true."

How is participation in the *risen* life of Jesus to be accomplished before our physical death? It may sound a bit silly, but the question is a real one. How do you participate in the promised future before it arrives? How do we *remember* the future? The early Christian community found the answer to those questions in its understanding of baptism. "Do you not know," asked Paul, "that all of us who have been baptized into Christ Jesus were baptized into his death? Therefore we have been buried with him by baptism into death, so that, just as Christ was raised from the dead by the glory of the Father, so we too might walk in newness of life" (Romans 6:3-4).

Water, of course, is the great biblical symbol of life and of the Spirit, the Breath of God. The biblical story comes out of a part of the world that is essentially a desert, and in a desert culture, water is life. Ancient baptismal prayers contained many allusions to water. There are the waters of the Genesis account of Creation, the waters of the Flood, the water of the womb, the rivers of paradise, the water from the rock in the desert during the Exodus, the water at the wedding feast of Cana, and the water flowing from the wounded side of the dying Jesus.

A contemporary baptismal liturgy offers an abbreviated version:

We thank you, Almighty God, for the gift of water. Over it the Holy Spirit moved in the beginning of creation. Through it you led the children of Israel out of their bondage in Egypt into the land of promise. In it your Son Jesus received the baptism of John and was anointed by the Holy Spirit as the Messiah, the Christ, to lead us, through his death and resurrection, from the bondage of sin into everlasting life.

We thank you, Father, for the water of Baptism. In it we are buried with Christ in his death. By it we share in his resurrection. Through it we are reborn by the Holy Spirit.[2]

While we live in a largely baptized society, relatively few of us can remember our own baptism. Many of us were baptized as infants, whether through cultural pressure or because of real faith on the part of our parents. Most would argue that though ours may be a baptized society, it is clearly not a Christianized one. True or not, the ubiquity of baptism makes it virtually impossible for us to understand the revolutionary difference the practice made in the life of converts during the church's early centuries. To be baptized meant a radical break with one's culture, family, friends, values, and lifestyle. It set you apart from all of these. You had to adopt a totally different worldview and, often, live in a totally different community. Perhaps the closest equivalent we can imagine in our day and age is the kind of change one makes when joining a religious order to become a monk or a nun.

When we read the story through the salvation lens, baptism is seen as our ticket to heaven, a means of getting saved. The Creation lens gives us an even larger picture:

> Great indeed is the baptism which is offered you. It is a ransom to captives; the remission of offenses; the death of sin; the regeneration of the soul; the garment of light; the holy seal indissoluble; the chariot to heaven; the luxury of paradise; a procuring of the kingdom; the gift of adoption.[3]

All of which might add up to an additional definition that says baptism is our way of celebrating the funeral for our old life. As someone has said, "Make sure you die before you die. There may not be time afterward."

Death

Obviously, physical death isn't part of the equation. But the expectation is that in baptism we'll renounce our former life—a life marked by sin, disobedience, and an inability to live a holy life—and embrace a totally new way of living and responding to the love of God. As we saw above, it's a matter of being identified with the death of Jesus. "Therefore we have been buried with him by baptism into death, so that, just as Christ was raised from the dead by the glory of the Father, so we too might walk in newness of life" (Romans 6:4). In earlier years a candidate for baptism was asked to renounce "the world, the flesh, and the Devil."

A modern version puts it this way:

> *Question:* Do you renounce Satan and all the spiritual forces of
>   wickedness that rebel against God?

Answer: I renounce them.

Question: Do you renounce the evil powers of this world which corrupt and destroy the creatures of God?

Answer: I renounce them.

Question: Do you renounce all sinful desires that draw you from the
   love of God?

Answer: I renounce them.[4]

It didn't take the church too long to develop a wonderfully dramatic form for acting out and proclaiming this kind of theology. Within a couple of centuries it was customary for candidates for baptism to be prepared for the event by months, or even years, of teaching and prayer. When the appointed time came, they were brought to the Christian assembly, to a place where there was an adequate supply of water. On one side of the pond, pool, or river, they would remove all of their clothing, as a symbol of stripping off the old life. They would be immersed (or buried) in the water proclaiming their faith in the Father, the Son, and the Holy Spirit, then be led to the other side where they would be clothed with a white robe, symbolizing the new life and the virtues of Christ. For obvious reasons of modesty, men would be baptized by men and women by women.

The next step would be to lead these newly baptized and newly clothed people to the chief elder, the bishop, who would "seal" the baptism by anointing them with oil and laying hands on their heads, welcoming them into the life of the Christian community. The oil, called *chrism,* reminded them that they were followers of the Anointed One, the Christ, or in Hebrew, the Messiah. And the laying on of hands, in addition to being a natural gesture of commissioning and friendship, symbolized the hands of a midwife or a physician placed on the head of an infant being drawn from its mother's womb as the baby emerged into a new and larger arena of life.

Few of us today have been baptized in such dramatic fashion. In my own church, with some laudable exceptions, the current notion seems to be, "Let's see if we can baptize this person without getting anyone wet!" A few drops on the forehead have to serve as a reminder of the all-engulfing waters—something that might be called a token of a symbol of a sign. Many people, having experienced a conversion later in life, feel that they have somehow been cheated and seek to be baptized again, this time by immersion.

I can certainly sympathize with them, although I don't believe the amount of water is an essential element in baptism. That would be something like prescribing the precise amount of bread and wine one needs to consume in order to receive Holy Communion. Nor do I believe that we need to be baptized again. All that's needed is for us to claim our baptismal inheritance, to make it our own, and to enter consciously into the lifestyle it presupposes. But for dramatic value, you simply can't beat total immersion. It *looks* like death and resurrection.

Some years ago I spoke at a church conference on the topic of baptism. During our closing Eucharistic celebration, we took bowls of water and, using pine branches, sprinkled the assembled worshipers as a reminder of their baptism. Among those present were a mother and her eight-year-old son with whom she had been having problems because of his habit of lying at school. When they returned home and school began again, the mother questioned the boy about his lying. He replied, "Oh, don't worry, Mom. God healed that when the bishop sprinkled us with water."

Regardless of the quantity of water, the old clothes are to be left on the other side. Naked we were born; naked we are born again. One of the problems that most of us face, however, is a sort of nostalgia for the old ways. Like the pilgrims in the desert, we often want to go back to Egypt. The old clothes, the old habits, seem to rise up, like something out of a

Disney cartoon, with a life of their own and beckon us from across the divide. "Surely you don't mean to abandon us *forever*," they seem to say— and we are all too willing to listen.

The old ways, the old habits, the old—dare I say it—sins, however destructive they may have been, were at least familiar. We had made an uneasy truce with them. And, as a result, living in the new is a daily challenge. Although it was made in a slightly different context, Paul's statement, "I die every day!" (1 Corinthians 15:31) is a good reminder of what it means to live the baptized life.

Into the Name

But there's more. Jesus sent his followers out to baptize "in the name of the Father and of the Son and of the Holy Spirit." When we do something "in the name" of another, that usually means we do it as the agent of the other person. In this case, however, the meaning is different and much deeper. In the original Greek, the preposition is not *in* but *into*. The imagery suggests that somehow or other we're baptized into the very nature of the Holy Trinity. It isn't simply a matter of becoming members of the Christian church, of sharing human companionship with like-minded believers, but of participation in the very life of God. The new family is where God's life is being lived out on earth. The early church fathers used a kind of shorthand phrase to describe what they found happening—"Jesus became what we are so that we might become what he is." The apostolic community could say, without a hint of self-righteousness, "It has seemed good to the Holy Spirit and to us" (Acts 15:28). And Paul could echo with such phrases as, "We have the mind of Christ" (1 Corinthians 2:16), and "It is no longer I who live, but it is Christ who lives in me" (Galatians 2:20). The language is organic rather than organizational. "The glory that you have given me I have given them," says Jesus, "so that they may be one, as we are one, I in them and you in me, that they may become completely one" (John 17:22-23).

This amazing indwelling was on John's mind when he wrote: "It is this which we have seen and heard that we declare to you also, in order that you may share with us in a common life, *that life which we share with the Father and his Son Jesus Christ*" (1 John 1:3, REB). And another example is found in the well-known Pauline benediction, "The grace of the Lord Jesus Christ, and the love of God, and fellowship in the Holy Spirit, be with you all" (2 Corinthians 13:14, NEB). The fellowship—better translated as "the sharing of a common life"—is part of the blessing.

These pictures of what the Christian church is designed to be may seem to be utopian, and perhaps they are. But the fact is that for millions of people, they've ceased to be fantasies and are becoming experiential realities.

Family

I had long believed in the central role that *koinonia* plays in the biblical story, but my beliefs had been largely theoretical. In other words, they were affirmations of what the biblical story said ought to be true, but I had only the barest minimum of experiential confirmation. There were a few fleeting glimpses of Christian community when I could see that some people seemed to enjoy a deeper level of fellowship than that provided by simply sharing a pew on a Sunday morning. A parishioner described this for me one day when he said, "I just realized that all of my closest friends, the people I really want to be with, are the same ones I go to church with."

My theoretical understanding began to take on an experiential dimension during the summer of 1973. My family and I visited the Church of the Redeemer in Houston, Texas, where God seemed to be doing some remarkable things. *Koinonia* wasn't just a theory or a belief, but a tangible commodity there. Several hundred people had developed a new form of Christian community, which was centered in a network of extended family households. Each household had both single and married people along with their children. Usually two or three people were the breadwinners, holding full-time jobs in order to provide for the rest of the household. The other adults were then free for full-time involvement in one or more of the church's many neighborhood ministries.

We spent a week staying in one of the households and participating in some of the church's activities. We also helped out in the large food-distribution program, went to meetings of various leadership and out-reach committees, and participated in some of the many opportunities for worship. Informal noonday Eucharistic celebrations attracted several hundred people, mostly young, and we were joined by more than a thousand worshipers at both the Friday night prayer and praise service and the Sunday Eucharist. The power of the Holy Spirit was evident everywhere, and the sense of deep Christian community was overwhelming. These were people who lived in church and went to the world rather than vice versa. Or to put it another way, the Christian community had become their primary community.

My theoretical understanding of the church as the body of Christ suddenly had a tangible reality to it so that I found myself thinking, *So* this *is what it looks like!* As I addressed the congregation at the end of the week, I said that I felt much like a paleontologist who, after years of piecing together a few ancient bones, is suddenly confronted with a living dinosaur. (And this was twenty years before *Jurassic Park!*)

One of the most amazing results of our visit was the enthusiasm of our children. They, too, had caught something of the vision that moved Redeemer and were fantasizing about how we might replicate the lifestyle in our own home. And this from kids who had previously fought tooth and nail for a room of their own! Barbara and I were fascinated too. But we thought that, realistically, nothing of that nature could happen until all our children were grown and gone and we had more freedom.

God seemed to have different plans. Within two months of our return home to Colorado, it seemed that God began dropping people on our doorstep and asking us to take them in, not as guests, but as members of the family. I don't know how to describe the process that led to our issuing the invitations. It was as simple a matter as my wife and me looking at each other and discovering that we each had the same idea. Before we knew what was happening, we found ourselves involved in a new expression of *koinonia,* of Christian community.

The first three recruits were my wife's mother who was suffering from advanced osteoporosis, an unmarried woman who had been ordained as a deacon in the Episcopal Church but was currently out of a job, and a young man who worked at my office. He was gay and was struggling to live a celibate life and felt he needed the support of a loving family in order to do that.

The initial months were difficult. Natural families have enough problems of their own without adding strangers to the mix. We had no blueprints, and we made many mistakes. In hindsight, we learned far more from the mistakes than from our few successes. As more people joined us, we had to move to a larger house. We found an old three-story house in the downtown area that had once been the home of a prominent Denver rabbi and later had been converted into a rabbit warren of small apartments. Doing the remodeling necessary to reconvert it into a family dwelling probably helped us more than any theological theory about community. Shared tasks can be wonderful community builders. By this time we numbered eighteen under the same roof, ranging in age from two to sixty-five.

Differences in temperament quickly surfaced, and each of us discovered previously unacknowledged areas of sin and selfishness that had to be brought to the light. We quickly learned that this was a necessary part of the process. The old had to die in order for the new to be born. God seemed to be on a search-and-destroy mission, exposing and tearing down those parts of our character that were inconsistent with his building plans.

A friend once told me that he had two hat racks by his front door. One he had labeled "hats" and the other "masks." We found that to work on being family required that we leave our masks at the door. After all, masks are artificial, and God doesn't bless artificiality. Faces are real. And meeting each other face to face brought a deeper sense of authenticity into our fellowship and made possible a greater degree of love for each other. We couldn't afford to remain strangers to each other, still less landlord and tenants, host and guests. We needed each other, and we found that each member had gifts that, when shared, turned out to be blessings for other members of the household.

A visiting bishop once asked me confidentially, "Just how many of the people here are spiritually well and able to give, and how many are sick and need to receive?" I replied, "We have eighteen of each—just who is in which category depends on the day you ask." The strong carry the weak, knowing that tomorrow or the next day the roles may be reversed.

We discovered that all the little tasks that go into making a large household function efficiently had to be equally valued and recognized. We developed a new vocabulary that saw every task as a form of ministry. We had the cooking ministry, the cleanup ministry, the laundry ministry, the bathroom-cleaning ministry, the grocery-shopping ministry, the furnace-room ministry, and lots more. If any one of these ministries suffered, all the others suffered too. While in the outside world I had many calls for my bishop's ministry, in the household I was more useful doing cooking and cleanup. My miter may have looked impressive in church, but it was useless at home!

We found that old values were being replaced by new ones. What was "mine" was assumed now to be "ours," including the bathroom! The most obvious effect of this understanding was economy of time, money, and human resources. Under the normal patterns of our society, we might have occupied five or six different households with all of their attendant expenses. This community arrangement made much more time and money available for outside projects. The compulsive acquisitiveness, so characteristic of our culture ("I shop, therefore I am") began to loosen its hold on our imaginations, and a simpler lifestyle was possible. Things began to matter much less and people much more.

And we began to relate to one another in a different fashion. I came home one evening and noticed a young woman mending a pair of my jeans. I thanked her and offered to take her turn at cleaning up after supper. She glanced up, smiled, and said, "You don't have to pay me back. This is the kingdom of heaven."

Kingdom of heaven it may have been, but it was and is far from paradise! We haven't yet found the way to eradicate original sin. Relationships are hard and require a lot of tending. And we often stumbled. We continued to pray and grope our way forward. We were, and still are, works in progress. The closer you get to each other, the easier it is to step on each other's toes. As a result, we quickly found that the mechanism for healing hurts—forgiveness—was something we had to master and use on a daily basis. We had to learn to forgive quickly and, equally important, we had to learn to stick to our decision to forgive. Unresolved conflicts and unforgiven injuries are two of the most toxic enemies of any true community.

Needless to say, many people in the Episcopal Church in Colorado began to wonder what was going on. There were references to "the bishop's commune," and more than a few people raised questions about the advisability of what we were doing. It wasn't the normal way for a bishop to behave! Some worried that my attention to the community would detract from my availability as diocesan pastor. As it turned out, it was the other way around. I had more time, more energy, and more productivity to offer, but it took several years for people to discover this.

Many of the questions and apprehensions disappeared in 1976 when Ann B. Davis, the actress who played "Alice" on *The Brady Bunch,* joined our community. Her television image (matched by her true character) was so wholesome and full of humor and common sense that people seemed to conclude that if she was part of the experiment, it must be all right! It wasn't long before "the bishop's commune" was replaced by "The Bishop's Bunch." And a visitor, the presiding bishop of the Episcopal Church at the time, once dubbed our household "The Bishop's Ark."

There are critics of a closely knit Christian community who feel that such arrangements mean a retreat from the needs of the world. We found that just the opposite was true. The awesome fact is that God has chosen to love the world *through* the church. She is meant to be God's vessel of social transformation, a working model, however imperfect, of the new humanity that God is creating, where "the blind recover their sight, the lame walk, the lepers are made clean, the deaf hear, the dead are raised to life, the poor are hearing the good news" (Matthew 11:5, NEB). Rediscovering some form of Christian *koinonia* is the only way the church can be faithful to its mission.

This is not the place for a lengthy chronicle of our life together. And I certainly don't offer it as a model for others to follow. In hindsight I believe it has been a kind of laboratory experiment designed to explore some of the blessings that close Christian fellowship can bring and to learn more of what Jesus meant when he said that where two or three are *gathered together* in his name, he will be in the midst of them.

The experiment has yielded some hopeful results. One of them is the validation of Jesus' words about losing your life in order to find it. We discovered great joy when we began to escape the getting-my-needs-met syndrome and began to focus on meeting the needs of others. We found that, despite the negative comments of cynics, the family can still be the agent of God's redemptive power for its own members and for outsiders as well. We welcomed a number of troubled families and individuals over the years and often saw a dramatic improvement in their own self-understanding, their ability to function, and their sense of hope for the future, without our having to *do* anything specific to bring about such results. And my wife's mother, whose physician had predicted that, because of her advanced osteoporosis, she would be in a wheelchair within a year of having joined us, lived with us sixteen years until she died. And she never needed the chair!

As a result, we became more and more convinced that real systemic transformation is possible. Many people in our culture are so jaded that they tell us that no deep change in our personalities is possible, that what passes for change and improvement is merely cosmetic. "The best indicator of future behavior is past behavior," they say. We found that the cynics are wrong.

There are many ways in which this new fellowship can be experienced, many ways in which common ordinary Christians can tap into the vast reservoirs of hope that Christian community offers. But they all have the same starting point—a decision to break the old pattern in which we live in the world and go to church. The beginnings may be found in such simple things as participation in a small Bible study or prayer group, becoming part of an outreach ministry such as a food pantry, visiting shut-ins, or working on a common project like building a Habitat house. All of these are simple ways to enter more deeply into the new creation, to make the Christian community our primary community so that we can live in the church and go to the world. And all of them are ways in which we can experience the warm embrace of the Father and hear afresh the wonderful good news that our Father loves us very much.

The important thing is to *get on board the Ark.*

Abbot Lot came to Abbot Joseph and said: Father, according as I am able, I keep my little rule, and my little fast, my prayer, meditation and contemplative silence; and according as I am able I strive to cleanse my heart of (evil) thoughts; now what more should I do? The elder rose up in reply and stretched out his hands to heaven, and his fingers became like ten lamps of flame. He said, Why not be totally changed into fire?

—ABBOT LOT, FOURTH CENTURY

THE NEW LAW

Unnatural Acts

Back in 1963 I spent a long afternoon in a closet. Not a metaphorical closet, but a real one. It was a long narrow space with a sharply slanted ceiling beneath a flight of stairs that my wife and I had set apart for private prayer.

I was in despair, trying to figure out just who and what I was and why I was where I was. A year before, the head of the missionary department of the Episcopal Church had discovered that I was fluent in Spanish and had urged me to take a post in Costa Rica. "There is a great need for your talents in San José," he said. I was extremely happy in my parish in New Mexico and had little desire to leave, but after a few more flattering comments about my "special gifts" that were "so desperately needed," I talked it over with my wife and decided to go.

When we arrived, I discovered that I had been hoodwinked. They had assigned me to an English-speaking chaplaincy congregation, and the local bishop didn't have a clue about my linguistic abilities. I felt betrayed. All of the reasons that had caused us to pull up our roots and make the move were apparently insignificant. Obviously it was too late to do anything about it, so we decided to make the best of a bad job and pray for something more appropriate in the months to come. But I didn't like it, and after about six months, my frustration finally boiled over—hence the afternoon in the closet.

I wanted to find out just how I had gotten into such a mess in the first place, and I realized I needed a time of real, brutally honest self-examination. I searched my heart, seeking my true motivations. Was I trying to obey God or was I trying to impress someone else? I looked as honestly as I knew how at my many sins, my vanity, my self-deceptions, pious poses, ecclesiastical game playing, fears, anxieties, lies, and conceits. It felt as though I were pawing my way through a garbage can.

After peeling off layer after layer of hypocrisy, I discovered one thing that wasn't the product of my own pride and wasn't infected by my usually mixed motives. It seemed to be free from all other entanglements, something genuine and true in its own right. It was a deep longing and desire to do those things that are pleasing to God. I felt as though I had found a bright shining jewel—a ruby perhaps—at the bottom of the garbage can. And the amazing thing was that I knew beyond the shadow of a doubt that I hadn't put it in there. It was nothing that I had manufactured. God had made it as a gift of sheer grace and somehow, when I wasn't looking, had sneaked it into my heart.

I think for years I had relied on my own natural abilities to serve God. My talents, my efforts, my discipline, my intelligence would be enough. Suddenly I realized how poor my own efforts had been and, at the same time, how cleverly God had anticipated my weakness and had supplied the one necessary thing.

That knowledge alone was sufficient to see me through the immediate crisis of faith and quite a number of subsequent ones. When I came out of that closet, I did so having had a convincing demonstration of something that heretofore I had known only in my head—that my human nature, unaided by God's grace, is simply not up to the job of living. I need something more, something that doesn't come naturally.

It isn't natural to be a Christian. We're not naturally loving, generous, kind, and forgiving. While God's original dream of the universe was that everything should be good, something happened to spoil that dream, and we're stuck with the consequences.

One of my high-school classmates became a writer of short stories, many of which appeared in the *New Yorker* magazine. I thought some of them were a little strange, but maybe that was because I didn't understand everything I read. I once saw an anthology of some of his works titled *Unspeakable Practices, Unnatural Acts,* and I remember thinking at the time that he'd either gone completely over the edge or he'd become a Christian.

You see, while "unnatural acts" could refer to something awful like unrestrained promiscuous fleshly vice, it could also refer to something really beautiful, like full-blown Christian virtue. For fallen creatures like us, there is nothing natural about being good. Virtue doesn't come naturally to us, and goodness is a struggle. "I do not do the good I want, but the evil I do not want is what I do," admitted Paul (Romans 7:19), and when we're honest, we know that he speaks for all of us, at least some of the time.

One of the subtlest deceptions of our time is the notion that, left to ourselves, we human beings will turn out pretty well. We're tempted to believe that if we can just eliminate all the bad external influences—the dragons and the wicked stepmothers of hunger, fear, injustice, and oppression—everything will be all right. The wolf will immediately lie down with the lamb, and we'll all live happily ever after. In the real world, the truth is much closer to Woody Allen's comment that the wolf and the lamb may lie down together, but the lamb won't get much sleep.

It isn't natural to forgive seventy times seven, to walk the extra mile, to turn the other cheek, to bless our persecutors, or to put the needs of others before our own desires. I always tell people that if they really want to commit an unnatural sexual act, they should get married and remain faithful to their spouse " 'til death us do part." Golden wedding anniversaries are worth celebrating precisely because they're such victories of unnatural behavior.

You'll remember that God gave Moses the Law because our "natural" behavior had become self-centered and destructive. Our family tree was traceable back to Adam and Eve, and, unfortunately, we had inherited too many of their family characteristics.

If "doing what comes naturally" were the same thing as doing what is right and virtuous, there would have been no need for the Law, no need for any moral or ethical teaching, certainly no need for divine commandments, and still less for the Incarnation. The whole world would be topsy-turvy. Sin, if the category could still be retained, would be the sort of behavior engaged in by people who acted contrary to their natural inclinations. Thus, we would criticize the brave who, contrary to nature, remain in dangerous surroundings to help others, and we would reward the cowards who, naturally, flee to save their own skins.

The long and the short of it is that moral and ethical behavior, as defined by the Law and the Prophets, as lived and taught by Jesus and as celebrated by the Christian community for two thousand years is *unnatural*. It is produced by a combination of grace and obedience overcoming our natural instincts in an attempt to model, if even for a brief Camelot-like moment, something of a *supernatural* lifestyle.

Jesus describes our natural condition when he says, "out of the heart come evil intentions, murder, adultery, fornication, theft, false witness, slander" (Matthew 15:19). And at the Last Judgment, those who have engaged in such "unnatural" acts as feeding the hungry, clothing the naked, and housing the homeless are the ones to hear, "Come, you that are blessed by my Father" (Matthew 25:34).

In the new creation, condemnation is reserved for what, in the fallen creation, has become natural, and praise is bestowed on the unnatural. "The works of the flesh [our natural or fallen humanity] are obvious: fornication, impurity, licentiousness" and so on, says Paul (Galatians 5:19-21). And praise is reserved for those who "have crucified the flesh with its passions and desires," and, therefore, produce the fruit of the Spirit [not the fruit of our natural impulses] such as "love, joy, peace, patience, kindness, generosity, faithfulness, gentleness, and self-control" (Galatians 5:22-23).

The fact that such virtues as courage, integrity, fidelity, and honesty are almost universally applauded is indicative of the value we place on unnatural activity. Courage has no meaning unless our natural tendency is to be cowardly, and fidelity is an empty word unless we're naturally unfaithful.

Transformation

I have a close friend who told me that he postponed making a major decision about his future vocation for ten years because of his uncertainty about the will of God. He wanted very much to make a change of direction, but at the same time he was deeply committed to doing what God wanted him to do. His working assumption was that if he wanted to do something so desperately, it must be contrary to the will of God! The ten-year struggle ended, he said, when he discovered that the reason he wanted the thing so much was because God had given him the desire to do it.

What would it be like to awaken one morning only to discover that your deepest desires have been transformed and that the thing you most wish to do is what God wants you to do? How would it feel to find yourself echoing the words of the psalmist and spontaneously uttering phrases like these?

I find my delight in your commandments, because I love them...
and I will meditate on your statutes! (Psalm 119:47-48)

Oh, how I love your law! It is my meditation all day long! (verse 97)

How sweet are your words to my taste, sweeter than honey to my
mouth! (verse 103)

Your decrees are my heritage forever; they are the joy of my heart!
(verse 111)

Reading the biblical story through the salvation lens, many Christians
have been eager to emphasize the New Testament's insistence that we aren't
saved *by* the Law. Our salvation is not a reward for our obedience to all of
the Law's demands. But that eagerness sometimes gives the impression that
we believe that we're saved *from* the Law. And further, since it is God's grace
and that grace alone that saves, the Law's demands may be set aside.

It's more than ironic that Jesus himself contradicts such a superficial
dismissal of the Law. "Do not think that I have come to abolish the law or
the prophets; I have come not to abolish but to fulfill" (Matthew 5:17).
The question then becomes, What does that mean? How does Jesus fulfill
the Law, and what does that mean for his disciples?

In popular Christian conversation, the relationship between Law and
grace is a troubled one. Unthinking Christians have all too often trivialized the Torah—the Law—by referring to it as "just a list of rules and regulations," thought to be outmoded or unnecessary now that Jesus has
come.

We only have to look at how Jesus interpreted the Law to see how
deeply he was immersed in it, how much he considered himself a man of

the Torah. Before hearing the Sermon on the Mount, we might have been able to imagine that we had kept the Law's demands if we hadn't literally murdered anyone or committed physical adultery. But after Jesus revealed the invisible root system of sin and pointed out, for example, that our anger at others is tantamount to murder and that the indulgence of lustful fantasies equals adultery, where can we hide?

Some tell us that the Law, especially as Jesus interprets it, is meant to demonstrate to us how far we are from being righteous, and therefore, how much we need God's forgiveness and grace. All well and good. But to jump from there to saying that once we've recognized our need for forgiveness, we can ignore the Law's demands is not only illogical but also contradictory to the whole of the New Testament story.

In the prologue to John's gospel, the author testifies that "from his [Jesus'] fullness we have all received, grace upon grace. The law indeed was given through Moses; grace and truth came through Jesus Christ" (John 1:16-17). This is John's way of saying the same thing that Matthew records Jesus as saying about fulfilling the Law. Not only the Old Testament, but human history itself demonstrates humanity's inability to live up to the demands of virtually any of our ethical and moral codes.

The biblical story offers us two apparently irreconcilable notions about the Law. On the one hand, there are powerful admonitions to keep the Law, and on the other hand, there are the many promises of forgiveness when we fail. "Unless your righteousness exceeds that of the scribes and Pharisees, you will never enter the kingdom of heaven," and "Be perfect, therefore, as your heavenly Father is perfect" are phrases that have haunted Christians for centuries. The burden of them is made tolerable only by setting them alongside Jesus' words to the paralytic, "Your sins are forgiven," or his tender remarks to the woman taken in adultery, "neither do I condemn you; go...and do not sin again." And the picture is completed by

Paul's insistence that we aren't justified by the works of the Law, but rather through faith in Jesus Christ.

Either of these polarities, taken by itself, can lead to disastrous results. Emphasizing the Law alone can easily lead us into one of two equally destructive behavior patterns. We can become narrow-minded, self-righteous bigots, too easily identified with those whom Jesus describes as trying to remove a speck from our neighbor's eye while ignoring the plank in our own, or we can lapse into total despair over our failures and give up completely. Emphasizing forgiveness alone can encourage a self-indulgent abdication of responsibility, assuming that whatever we do, "God will forgive; after all, that's his job."

The Creation lens offers a third alternative. In the new creation, God's commands become God's enablings. "Grant what you command, and command what you will," said Saint Augustine in his *Confessions*. God ceases to be seen as a distant moralist, watching our feeble attempts to live righteously. The act of Creation is an exercise of power, and new creation is not simply metaphorical. It, too, is an exercise of the power of God. Through the Creation lens we can see that power working with us and in us to transform our behavior by transforming our hearts. In other words, we aren't left on our own in the struggle against sin, Satan, and death. There's someone on our side.

Location, Location, Location

The prophetic promises are beginning to be fulfilled, and you'll remember that the promises relating to the Law were about *location, location, location.*

> I will make a new covenant with the house of Israel and the house
> of Judah. It will not be like the covenant that I made with their
> ancestors when I took them by the hand to bring them out of the

land of Egypt—a covenant that they broke, though I was their husband, says the LORD. But this is the covenant that I will make with the house of Israel after those days, says the LORD: *I will put my law within them, and I will write it on their hearts;* and I will be their God, and they shall be my people. No longer shall they teach one another, or say to each other, "Know the LORD," for they shall all know me, from the least of them to the greatest, says the LORD; for I will forgive their iniquity, and remember their sin no more. (Jeremiah 31:31-34)

And,

I shall give you a new heart and put a new spirit within you; I shall remove the heart of stone from your body and give you a heart of flesh. I shall put my spirit within you and make you conform to my statutes; you will observe my laws faithfully.... You will be my people and I shall be your God. (Ezekiel 36:26-28, REB)

So long as the Law remains external to us, a moral code imposed from above, it seems to produce more guilt than grace, and the best response we can make looks like a series of brief and sporadic attempts at obedience. Even when we're convinced about the Law's validity and the rightness of its demands, we feel ourselves laboring under a handicap when we strive to keep it. Let the theologians debate whether our weakness, our propensity to put ourselves at the center of our own universes—in short, our original sin—is hereditary or environmentally conditioned. The fact remains that, just as in Eden, there's a snake in our garden, too, and as we noted earlier, we do tend to behave like our original parents. So far as we can tell, no one escapes. Human nature *is* evenly distributed.

The promise of the prophets is that God will relocate the Law. Jeremiah hears God say that he will write it on our hearts. Ezekiel hears the Lord promise a new heart, presumably with the Law already inscribed upon it. In modern terms it's like some new software added to our hard drive—a new program that offers to improve the way our system operates. The new location is the human heart. But just what does that mean?

In our culture we're accustomed to speaking of the heart as the seat of our emotions. Not so the Bible. In biblical terms, the functions we ascribe to head and heart are each moved down one level. We think with our heads and feel with our hearts. Biblical authors thought with their hearts and felt with their gut. When the New Testament describes Jesus as "being moved with compassion," it wasn't his heart that was being squeezed, but his stomach. The actual word in Greek means something like having labor pains or stomach cramps.

But there's more. Biblically, the heart is more than just the thinking apparatus, the conscious mind. It represents the inner core of a person's being, the action center, the place where all the real decisions are made. It includes what psychologists might call the subconscious as well as the conscious. Hence, to say that the Law will be written on the heart is a promise of a radical internal transformation in which we find our wills being influenced by the will of God. In other words, the promise is that we'll awaken one day with a deep, burning desire to live as God wills. We'll clamber out of bed in the morning anxious to find fresh ways of worshiping the Lord and loving our fellow human beings.

A note of caution is appropriate here. This isn't magic, but grace. New creation is indeed an exercise of power, *but not of overwhelming power.*

It would be nice to be able to say that this transformation happens automatically, that God takes over so powerfully that we simply can't resist. I confess that I have certainly prayed that way on many occasions—"Take my life, God, and you make all the decisions." But that prayer—which is really an attempt to escape responsibility—has never been answered. I have yet to become God's robot, programmed in such a way that my resistance is automatically overruled. The truth is that God will not magically take over the management of our life, but God *will* tip the scales ever so slightly. The balance of power will be shifted just enough to enable us to say yes to God and no to sin. But that "just enough" is enough to reduce our addiction to those things that we know are harmful to our spiritual well-being and the well-being of others.

A personal example. Addictions are, by definition, compulsions, things we can't *not* do. They are urgings that we say yes to simply because we aren't free to say no to them. There was a time in my own life when I was so addicted to sleeping pills and excessive amounts of alcohol that I would literally anesthetize myself at night in order to go to sleep. It was not a healthy lifestyle! But then one evening, as I was pouring a large amount of brandy into a glass, I realized that something had happened inside me and the power of the compulsion had been broken. I suddenly knew that I didn't need it. It wasn't a feeling that I could conquer my addiction by greater exercise of will power, by trying a little bit harder. It was more like a clear awareness that the addiction had somehow been drained of its power to rule over me. I attributed it to a quiet exercise of God's grace, an unexpected gift of strength, and for the first time in years I was able to make a truly free decision about what I put into my body. I could still say yes to the drugs and alcohol, but now I could also say no to them. I didn't *need* them. The balance of power had been altered just enough to enable me to choose what I really wanted to choose. And the next day I discovered that the same thing had happened with regard to my addiction to tobacco.

Neither of these changes was brought about by an overwhelming exercise of divine power. It was more a gentle, loving nudge, like the slight midcourse correction that scientists give a spacecraft to ensure its proper

trajectory and speed it on to its appointed destination. It was barely noticeable to anyone but me. As my behavior began to change, however, it became noticeable to those who knew me.

Sin *101*

The Christian gospel is essential to the recovery of hope precisely because
it offers the forgiveness of sin. And forgiveness is par excellence an act of
new creation. It mends a broken friendship and resurrects one that was
dead. It creates and establishes a new relationship between God and us, a
relationship that we can trust and build upon. It heals the estrangement
and deals with the fragmentation and alienation so characteristic of lives
separated from the goodness of God.

Paul speaks with great compassion about those people who are "without hope and without God in the world" (Ephesians 2:12, NIV). The
notion of forgiveness is so central to the core teaching of the New Testament that Christians have enshrined it in the brief summaries of biblical
teaching known as the creeds. And in the creeds it stands with the other
signs of the new creation. "I believe in the forgiveness of sins, the resurrection of the body, and the life everlasting." All hope of heaven hinges on
God's final forgiveness. The good news is that we may *remember* that ultimate blessing, borrow some of that future, and live in its glory today.

There was a time in the history of the church when the offer of divine
forgiveness was received by outsiders with immense excitement and grati-
tude, as something almost too good to be true. I caught a glimpse of the
raw power of such an offer several years ago. I was in a small Bible study
group with a man who had been a German U-boat commander during
World War II. He'd had a remarkable career that ended when his subma-
rine was sunk in the Atlantic, and he spent the rest of the war in an Allied

prisoner-of-war camp. One evening during a coffee break, he approached me and said, "Father, we Christians believe in the forgiveness of sins, don't we?" I assured him that we did. "That means all sins, doesn't it?" he continued. I said that it did, and with a haunted look in his eyes he spoke again, "*All* sins, *whatever* they might have been?" Looking at his face and hearing the imploring tone in his voice, I realized that his question was not the result of idle intellectual curiosity. It had a sense of desperation mingled with a cautious hope. While my imagination conjured up images of his having machine-gunned the lifeboats of sinking ships, I replied, "Yes, Dieter, *all* sins!" With a deep sigh of relief, he wiped his brow, turned away, and muttered, "Ach, t'ank Gott! T'ank Gott!"

If this truth seems to lack the power it once had in the proclamation of the Christian faith, it may be because in our culture's scramble to feel good about ourselves and raise our self-esteem, the very notion of sin and guilt has been pushed offstage. Several years ago, in an article describing the return of many baby boomers to church and synagogue, *Newsweek* magazine said, "In their efforts to accommodate, many clergy have simply airbrushed sin out of their vocabulary."

Benjamin Franklin said that the most important thing he had ever learned was that he was accountable to God. While that might sound like a frightening discovery, it's really good news. To be accountable for anything means, first of all, that you *count,* that you have dignity and are valued by someone, that you're important in the infinite scheme of things. That's a truly awesome thought. To believe in a God who doesn't hold us accountable would be to believe in a God who doesn't care.

We miss the whole point when we try to flee responsibility by explaining away our "antisocial behavior" or our "acting out"—the phrases themselves are attempts to sanitize sin and guilt—by blaming our heredity, environment, our genes, or bad toilet training. Equally useless is our

attempt to project our sense of guilt on other people or on external circumstances—an unjust society, abusive or absentee parents, dysfunc-
tional family systems, inadequate affirmation, and so on. All of these
attempts to escape accountability may help for a while, but in the long
run, they leave us with our pain intact. They don't deal with the root
problem.

A psychiatrist once told me that he had many days when he felt he
ought to be ordained a priest. He said that while his patients ostensibly
were seeking a deeper understanding of their behavior, he sensed that what
they really needed and what so many of them were unconsciously asking
for was absolution. "Even if they don't use the language," he told me, "they
want their sins forgiven."

The word *sin* gets a lot of bad press. We've come to associate it with
a sense of condemnation and a judgmental spirit. When I label some
form of behavior sinful, a frequent response is something like, "Why are
you condemning people who do that?" Ironically, to call any form of
behavior sinful is an act of hope, not an act of condemnation. The gospel
has a powerful and specific remedy for sin—forgiveness—but it has no
such relief for heredity or environment. It's something like the physician
who told her patient that she had no cure for the common cold, but to
come back when it turned into pneumonia because she had a remedy for
that.

Sin is shorthand for a wide variety of activities and, in some cases,
inactivities. There are sins of commission and sins of omission. But why
is it so important, and why does God look on it with such disfavor? I got
a clue one day when I was having a discussion with a family therapist. I
asked him how he and his associates dealt with the really tough marital
cases, the ones where there seemed to be little hope for reconciliation
between husband and wife. He thought for a moment then said, "Well,

we almost never recommend divorce." Then he seemed to remember who he was talking to and continued, "Not because we think divorce is a sin, Bishop, but because so many people get hurt in the process." I waited two beats then replied, "Bingo! You've just defined sin. Sin is what hurts people."

Biblically speaking, God's anger is aimed at sin because sin is whatever defaces, demeans, diminishes, or destroys his handiwork. In the same way that we get angry with those things or those people who hurt the ones we love, so God's wrath is directed toward those behaviors that hurt the ones he loves. If God's dream is that all his creatures know his love and live with one another in true shalom (justice, joy, equity, mercy, reconciliation, and peace), what other attitude could God take? We're tempted to think that God's wrath is a denial of his love when, in fact, just the opposite is true. What kind of love could stand by passively and watch while people are harmed or harm one another? Give me a passionate God who cares and gets angry!

In other words, when Scripture or the church labels some activity sinful, they do so for the same reason the surgeon general puts warning labels on cigarette packages: "This behavior has been proven to be harmful to your health and the health of those around you." To put it another way, discovering, identifying, and taking responsibility for sin is a therapeutic activity. It promotes the physical and spiritual health that God offers through forgiveness and enables us to enter ever more deeply into the new creation.

Forgiveness does not minimize the gravity of sin. If anything, it magnifies sin's seriousness by implying that the thing simply cannot be overlooked. It must be *overcome*. And the gospel story of the Cross graphically describes the cost of such forgiveness. With a brand-new beginning, a new creation can begin, and the future is filled with hope.

Reality Testing

In the Episcopal Church, one of the major privileges of bishops is that of celebrating Confirmation. After people reaffirm their baptismal promises, the bishop lays his or her hands on the candidate's head and prays. There's a choice of two brief prayers that ask for an increase of the power of the Holy Spirit in the lives of those being confirmed:

Strengthen, O Lord, your servant N. with your Holy Spirit; empower *him* for your service; and sustain him all the days of *his* life. *Amen.*

Or this:

Defend, O Lord, your servant N. with your heavenly grace, that she may continue yours forever, and daily increase in your Holy Spirit more and more, until she comes to your everlasting kingdom. *Amen.*

After doing this for a number of years, I began asking those being confirmed to write me letters describing what was different in their lives as a result of their fresh commitment to the baptismal covenant. I wanted to keep track of what God was doing. After all, we weren't "playing church." When the Christian community gathers and prays, it should expect something to happen. When we expect little or nothing to happen, we generally get what we expect. Worse, prayer without expectation can quickly become a meaningless ritual, the rote repetition of empty phrases. And it's dangerously close to thumbing your nose at the commandment that forbids taking the Lord's name in vain.

A covenant, after all, is a two-sided agreement. In this case, we make promises to God because God already has made promises to us. I wanted to know what was going on in the lives of those for whom we prayed. And keeping in touch with many of those I had confirmed, I began to see some remarkable results. People reported experiencing new dimensions in their relationship with God and with other people.

Sometimes it was simple and practical, as when a teenage boy told me that he had "stopped bugging his little sister." My reaction was, "How wonderful! Somewhere, some little girl is experiencing the love of God from a totally unexpected source—her big brother!"

Sometimes the witness was profound and moving, as in the case of a woman who had been raped who told me of a glorious transformation that had taken place in her life. She was no longer a "victim." When she was assaulted, she said, she had "learned the meaning of horror." "But with time," she continued, she had "learned also that as tightly as my attacker held my wrists, God held my hands, helped to dry my tears, and felt, really felt, my pain."

Another woman told me of the changes that were occurring at home: "As for my marriage, the trials and upset are being handled with a more gentle touch of both tongue and emotion through a solid commitment that my husband and I are married for life (boy was that a tough one!) and we'll grow to be one flesh in our Lord."

A teenager wrote, "I want my brother to know that I truly love him and that Christ loves him even more. I will be more affectionate to him as well as the rest of my family. I will let my father into my life, let him know who I am. I'll show more respect to my mother, and to my sister. I'll let God's love shine through me as an attempt to bring her back to Him."

A woman wrote of "something glorious" happening in her life. She said she was suspicious of feelings and emotions ("they're great, but they make a poor foundation"), but nonetheless, "every cell in my body leapt with life." She said that although she wasn't a "Pentecost type," she had received the gift of tongues at her Confirmation, a "gift of praying in an incomprehensible language. If I don't speak it, I think it. It's like a pent-up urgent hunger to reach God." She reported that her husband, too, had changed. "He has a growing faith that even day-to-day life in a giant corporation can no longer trample down."

A businessman told me, "I've spent a good share of my life wasting my time on *things,* material mostly, and the rest of the time on myself. This year I've realized that there is something greater than all. That one is God. He has helped me rid myself of my selfishness and sins.... Each day is a new and brighter adventure in life. Oh! What a nice change from the waste!"

A widow described "the certainty that I am not alone anymore.... It's not just me and the cat! There is a Presence, even in this room. God's love in the slightly dusty afternoon light. And if God is here, God can be anywhere.... How can I not be changed? I try to carry this tiny, smudged understanding with me, to polish it and make it a window, to focus the world in its frame."

Years of hearing and reading testimonies like these encouraged me so much that I began to offer candidates a "lifetime warranty" on their Confirmation. (One bright young lawyer suggested that I might want to guarantee parts only and not labor!) What I meant was that I expected that God would act in such a way that people would know that things were beginning to be different, not just in their "religious life," but in their life. I expected to see some evidence that their lives were beginning to be transformed, that they were discovering that, little by little, the desires of their hearts were starting to reflect what God wants from us. And I wasn't disappointed. The Law in the heart is less like a system of rules and more like the law of gravity. It is, as Thomas Merton said, "an entirely new spiritual reality." And spiritual realities are created by the Holy Spirit, the breath that God breathed into Adam in the first Creation and the breath that Jesus breathed into his disciples in the new. When the Law is written in the heart, when the heart of stone is replaced by one of flesh, wonderful things begin to happen. The old life passes away and the new one begins.

Empowerment

It's disconcerting for a preacher to hear his or her stock in trade equated with faultfinding and criticism. "I don't need any of your sermons" and "Don't start preaching to me" are common defenses against anyone who tries to offer advice. Granted, there are enough preachers who seem to specialize in scolding and chiding to have provided the caricature. You know the sort—the ones who delight in reminding us just how far we are from perfection without offering any solution other than "Strive more diligently!"

But the original meaning of preaching in the New Testament is proclamation, and the proclamation is about what God has done, is doing, and will do. The proclamation is *for* us but not *about* us. If there's any mention of improved behavior on our part, the improvement is seen to be the result of and the response to God's prior action. Preaching is not simply one more reminder that we need to try a little harder; it's rather a proclamation of God's power.

And the power has a name: Holy Spirit. The *Ruach,* to use the Hebrew term, or *Pneuma,* to use the Greek, is not thought of in impersonal terms like *the Force* in the *Star Wars* epic. This Spirit has personality and is equated with God's own self as God indwells and empowers human personality.

In Luke's gospel the risen Christ tells his disciples to wait until they receive this power before launching out on their global mission. "I am sending upon you what my Father promised; so stay here in the city until you have been clothed with power from on high" (Luke 24:49). And in the Acts of the Apostles, Luke reiterates the same message: "While staying with them, he ordered them not to leave Jerusalem, but to wait there for the promise of the Father. 'This,' he said 'is what you have heard from me; for John baptized with water, but you will be baptized with the Holy Spirit not many days from now'" (Acts 1:4-5).

Remember that this was a community that had heard Jesus teach, witnessed him perform signs and wonders, watched him die, and seen him resurrected. Despite all this, they still needed something more. For all of their knowledge, they weren't yet fully equipped for the mission with which they were charged. The fullness of the Christian life is not produced by information and learning alone, but by an infusion of power that converts the learning into glorious experience. And the wonder of it all is that the gift is ours for the asking. "Ask, and it will be given you.... Everyone who asks receives.... If you then, who are evil, know how to give good gifts to your children, how much more will the heavenly Father give the Holy Spirit to those who ask him!" (Luke 11:9,10,13).

If the Christian community, the new Ark, has power to offer healing and hope, it's because it is a Spirit-filled community. It isn't simply a gathering of like-minded people, but a gathering of people whose lives are being remolded by the Holy Spirit. According to Paul, the Holy Spirit working deep within us enables us to make two of the most important telling and hope-filled statements of the Christian faith.

The first is that intimate form of address Jesus gave us for God: Abba, "dear, loving Father." "For you did not receive a spirit of slavery to fall back into fear, but you have received a spirit of adoption. When we cry, 'Abba! Father!' it is that very Spirit bearing witness with our spirit that we are children of God" (Romans 8:15-16). And the second is the creed of the first-generation Christian church, "Jesus is Lord." "No one can say 'Jesus is Lord' except by the Holy Spirit" (1 Corinthians 12:3).

Abba is more than a form of address, more than the opening word of the Lord's Prayer. It speaks less about language and more about relationship and attitude. It's a reminder of just where we stand with regard to God and what God's attitude toward us really is. When the Holy Spirit convinces us, deep inside, that we are powerfully and eternally loved by the One who brought all things into being, our entire outlook on life is transformed. It's the sort of change alluded to in Jesus' parable of the prodigal son. The son comes home, you'll recall, hoping for little more than a grudging tolerance on the part of the father. "Make me as one of your hired servants" was his intended plea. Instead, he found himself overwhelmed by a lavish love that knew no bounds. A Scottish theologian describes it this way:

> The robe which is the garment of sonship is accompanied by the ring which is the insignia of authority and the sandals that distinguish the free man from the slave. The son who comes home is invited back into his lost inheritance, to delight again in his father's goodness and to rejoice.[1]

His expectation of having to call his father "My master" is replaced by the privilege of saying "Abba, my father."

When we see ourselves in a different light, we must also come to see others in a different light. During the dark days of the apartheid regime in South Africa, Desmond Tutu, speaking to a group of white Afrikaner businessmen, said, "My fervent wish for you is that one day you will come to know just how much God loves each of you. For when you comprehend that, you will be able to see how much God loves other people as well." It's easy to see why the Holy Spirit is eager to enable us to cry, "Abba, Father!"

But we are bold enough to address God in such intimate terms only because of the authority of the One who told us to do so. Jesus is Lord. Our profession of faith is the acting out of Paul's Trinitarian blessing. It's the grace of our Lord Jesus Christ, which reveals and demonstrates the love of God (the Father) and invites us into the communion—the shared life—of the Holy Spirit.

The Holy Spirit is the One who turns Law into grace, who enables us to become "doers of the word, and not merely hearers" (James 1:22). Doers of the Word are those who have entered into that holy partnership with the living God, a covenant relationship in which they move from being merely servants of God to being God's beloved children and fellow workers together with Christ. They're the ones who, to use C. S. Lewis's phrase, perform "those holy acts whereof 'God did it' and 'I did it' are both true descriptions."

Or, to use a lovely Spanish phrase, *Donde huelgan las palabras, comienza la danza*—"Where words come to an end, the dance begins!"

Take…the sword of the Spirit, which is the word of God.
—EPHESIANS 6:17

Indeed, the word of God is living and active, sharper than any two-edged sword, piercing until it divides soul from spirit, joints from marrow; it is able to judge the thoughts and intentions of the heart.
—HEBREWS 4:12

The truths of Holy Scripture…adapt themselves to each succeeding age, and portions long neglected, or but partially understood, break forth often with new energy when circumstances call for their application.
—ROBERT PAYNE SMITH

It is impossible to mentally or socially enslave a Bible-reading people.
—HORACE GREELEY

SEVEN

THE NEW SWORD

Armed and Dangerous

When we lived in Guatemala, my job called for a lot of travel outside the country. I developed a kind of good-natured game with the customs inspectors each time I returned to the Guatemala City airport. They would always ask if I had brought back anything subversive in my luggage, and my stock reply was, "Only the Bible." They always laughed. How little they knew!

In 1971 a handful of Christians and I made a public statement encouraging peaceful negotiations in Guatemala's undeclared civil war. Within a couple of days, we received a message from the country's vice president. It advised us to stick to reading our Bibles and to stay out of affairs that didn't concern us. We replied that reading our Bibles was what made us speak out in the first place. He was not amused, and within two weeks I was expelled from the country. A military dictatorship, with all its troops and weapons, felt threatened by a word of truth from some otherwise powerless people.

There are few things more subversive than the Bible, and it's no wonder that the Word of God is likened to a double-edged sword. Taken seriously, the Scriptures will subvert all our worldviews, our pretenses, and our value systems. The Bible tears down all our defenses and sits in judgment on all our personal and social game playing. While that may sound like a threat, it's really a promise. The new building cannot be erected until the old one is torn down. The Bible is, like the God who inspired it, merciless to hypocrisy but infinitely merciful to those who have the courage to abandon their disguises and stand naked and vulnerable to the light of God's gaze.

But such a blessing seems to be reserved for those who take the time to learn God's language and to hear what God is saying. What Mark Twain said about great literature can be applied even more poignantly to the Bible: "Those who *don't* read it are no better off than those who *can't* read it." In the final analysis, ignorance of the Scriptures is ignorance of God. The recovery of hope depends in large measure on our knowledge of what God is doing.

The Language of God

In 1961, when I was serving as rector of the Episcopal Church in Los Alamos, New Mexico, I learned that a prominent theologian, who also had impressive scientific credentials, was visiting nearby in Santa Fe. I immediately invited him to give a lecture to my congregation, which had a large number of nuclear scientists and engineers.

The title of his lecture was "The Language of God," and in a masterful presentation on a Saturday night, he had all of us pretty well convinced that God's language is mathematics. As I recall, he spoke about the mathematical precision found in certain parts of the universe, the strong force and the weak force in the atom, the periodic table of elements, and who knows what else. As I looked around the room, I could see heads nodding everywhere and big smiles on the faces of most of the scientists. I thought it was a great success.

But when I got home I began to think a bit more deeply. If mathematics is the language of God, where does that leave those of us who don't speak the language? I'm not illiterate, but I am, as a friend once told me, "innumerate." My math ended with high-school algebra and geometry. If God speaks mathematics, then he must not wish to communicate with very many people. I finally resolved the problem by concluding that mathematics may be what God speaks in *creation,* but that he uses a different language altogether for *revelation.*

The biblical story is truly about a God who communicates, a God who speaks, One who reveals his presence and purposes in unmistakable fashion. God speaks the universe into being, and once it's there, he speaks directly to the humans who exercise stewardship over the earth. God names and identifies himself, and throughout the story, we see him speaking directly to chosen people and indirectly through the prophets. We saw that it was the Creative Word who brought the universe into being, and we saw what that Creative Word did when it became flesh in Jesus. The real language of God is *story,* and specifically, the *biblical* story. Until we become familiar with that story, we can only make guesses about God's character, about his dreams and hopes for us and for the rest of creation.

A prominent theologian tells me that the most common form of apostasy—denial or rejection of the Christian faith—is the refusal to identify God with the God of Israel. If the One we call God is not the God of Abraham, Isaac, and Jacob, the One who rescued the slaves from the land of Egypt, formed them into his own people in the wilderness, and led them into the land of promise, then just who is God?

Our culture encourages us to define "God" in any way we wish, any way that "meets our needs." The result is a kind of theological anarchy, a mob scene where real conversation becomes impossible because of the totally different, and often contradictory, meanings ascribed to the word *God.* It may be that the time has come for those who wish to speak of the God of the Bible to use the name by which biblical people knew him: *Yahweh.* That, at least, would avoid some of the confusion.

John Calvin said that the human heart is an "idol factory." When we reject the God of the Scriptures, we inevitably create a series of what one of my friends calls "designer gods"—boutique deities fashioned out of our own imaginations to meet our fluid and fickle needs and desires. We might, for example, create a warlike god to bless our exercises of power and damn our enemies, an ethnic god to convince ourselves that our nation or tribe is really the best. We might fashion a prosperity god to bless our investments and promise us success, a pantheistic god to tell us that the universe is divine and so are we, or a radical feminist god to correct the very real evils of male chauvinism and patriarchal domination. The list goes on, and any number can play.

The only problem is that such gods are as homemade as any image fashioned out of wood or metal, and if we're not careful, we'll become idolaters, kneeling at the shrines of our own limited imaginations.

The biblical story was written to help us avoid such shallow thinking. It was written for our blessing and our benefit. Or, as Paul put it, "Whatever was written in former days was written for our instruction, so that by steadfastness and by the encouragement of the scriptures we might have hope" (Romans 15:4).

Losing Our Memory

It's no secret that our biblical memory has been eroding for almost a century. There was a time when the biblical story, all the way from Adam and Eve to the picture of the new heaven and new earth in Revelation, was the common family story of Western civilization. Knowledge of the story was considered essential to a person's education, whether or not the knowledge resulted in practical obedience and belief. The Bible wasn't thought to be the private property of either church or synagogue, but rather, part of the public domain. It was a book with which every educated person was familiar. A speaker or a writer could evoke its pictures, its images, and its stories with a mere word or a phrase. No need to go into detail.

In earlier days you had but to mention such things as selling your birthright for a mess of pottage, the valley of the dry bones, walking on water, a prodigal son, or a good Samaritan, and most people knew what you were talking about. For example, Helen Keller could use biblical images to describe the arrival of her teacher, Anne Sullivan:

> Thus I came up out of Egypt and stood before Sinai, and a power divine touched my spirit and gave it sight, so that I beheld many wonders. And from the sacred mountain I heard a voice which said, "Knowledge is love and light and vision."[1]

Obviously, such common consciousness of the biblical story has disappeared, even to the point of one person's having written a letter to the editor complaining that "those Christians" were trying to spoil the "spirit of Christmas" by bringing Jesus into it!

My own awareness of the growth of our culture's biblical amnesia remained largely theoretical for many years. I think I was naive and lulled into complacency because so many people *owned* Bibles. Biblical illiteracy was something we preachers were expected to make occasional scolding comments about, a phenomenon we were expected to "view with alarm" when the occasion demanded. But one night, in a British theater, I began to see it from a totally different perspective.

It was the summer of 1978, and my wife, Barbara, and I were in London visiting some friends. I was preparing to attend the Lambeth Conference, an international gathering of Anglican bishops that takes place every ten years. This particular summer, the British actor Alec McCowan was performing *St. Mark's Gospel* on the London stage. I had read a favorable review of the performance in the *New York Times,* and I was anxious to see it.

I had written to the archbishop of Canterbury, suggesting that he might try to arrange a production of *St. Mark* for the conference. As it turned out, greater minds had gotten there before me, and arrangements had already been made for a private performance of the play at Kent University, Canterbury, where the bishops were meeting.

Barbara and I didn't know that, however, so just to be on the safe side, we hastened to a West End theater to make sure we didn't miss the play. I'm glad we did, or I would have missed my "revelation." What sparked it wouldn't have happened in the midst of an audience of bishops.

The production itself was remarkable. McCowan came on stage, dressed somewhat informally. His only props were a table, a chair, a pitcher of water, and a glass. He gave a few introductory remarks, mostly about what modern scholars say about the origin and the particular character of Mark's gospel. With a twinkle in his eye, he even offered the old pious speculation, which I had heard in my seminary days, that the account of the young man who followed Jesus to his judgment dressed only in a sheet, then ran home naked when somebody snatched it away, might have been the writer's way of signing his work. Then, without warning, he launched into an animated recitation of the *King James Version* of the text.

The theater was packed and the performance was electrifying. My mind automatically compared the full theater to the many nearly empty churches I had seen in London. Despite the mesmerizing effect of the play, one part of my mind kept saying, *These people around us are theatergoers, not churchgoers (although one can be both at the same time), and they've paid good money just for the privilege of listening to the gospel. Why can't the church be that compelling and exciting?*

We were seated next to a young couple, probably in their thirties. They seemed to be enchanted by the performance. We exchanged pleasantries during the intermission, which served to confirm my suspicion that they were not drawn to the play by any conscious spiritual longing, but because they wanted to see good theater.

The lights dimmed and the second act began. You'll remember that toward the end of his gospel, Mark tells of several run-ins between Jesus and some hostile questioners. In one such encounter, where some Pharisees and Herodians try to trick Jesus into incriminating himself in a dispute about the legitimacy of paying taxes to a foreign emperor ("Is it lawful to give tribute to Caesar or not?"), Jesus asks his adversaries to show him the coin used for tribute. He then asks whose "image and superscription" is on it. They reply, "Caesar's." At this point, McCowan continued with the old familiar phrase, "Render therefore unto Caesar the things that are Caesar's, and unto God the things that are God's." The young woman beside me gasped audibly, grasped her companion's arm, and in a stage whisper said, "What a wonderful reply!"

I suddenly realized two things. First, she'd never heard the story before, and second, when she did hear it, she was *excited!*

My first reaction was envy. What would it be like, as an adult, to hear the gospel story for the first time? How would it sound to virgin ears, to ears that didn't automatically associate it with a list of "familiar quotations," Sunday-school memory verses, red-letter editions of the New Testament, or with a few poorly remembered fragments of old and possibly misleading sermons? Many people have at least some fuzzy notion about the biblical story—something about Adam and Eve in a garden, eating an apple, which, for some reason or another, was terribly upsetting to God; maybe Cain killing Abel; a bit about Noah and an ark; Moses (or was it Charlton Heston?) leading a huge mob of people through the Red Sea; David and

Goliath; maybe Joshua, who "fit the battle of Jericho"; Jonah and the whale, all of which was followed by Jesus; the Christmas stories; some healing and some teaching, which, though we don't remember the details, was awfully important; walking on the water; being crucified; and, they say, raised from the dead. But for this woman, the whole thing seemed to be new.

I began to wonder, *How did first-century audiences respond when someone read or told them the story?* Not just that particular story, but the whole story of Jesus? What would it be like to hear it without presupposition or prejudice? Would we be able to sense the drama, the lightning flashes of Jesus' wit as he sliced through the prejudices and presuppositions of his age? Would we recognize the finely tuned theological intellect that enabled him to teach, not in "familiar quotations," but as the people said, "with authority"? Would we sense the drama of the building tension caused by his popularity and the threat that that popularity posed to those in power? Would we share the worry of his mother and brothers and sisters that these ideological conflicts would inexorably lead to his death? Would we smile at the often humorous descriptions of slow-witted apostles, and would we have our hearts moved by the tenderness of one who went out of his way to spend time with the forgotten and marginalized?

My second reaction to the woman's response was excitement. It was nothing like a lightning bolt, but more like the "still, small voice" saying that there has probably never been a more urgent time, nor a better time for that matter, for the retelling of the biblical story. Biblical ignorance is not primarily a problem, but a great opportunity.

Obviously, most of us cannot pretend that we haven't read the story before, or at least sizable portions of it, and so reading it as if for the first time is impossible. But the primary thrust of this work and the reason for attempting to read it through the Creation lens is to get as close to such an experience as possible.

The Power of Story

By speaking story, God avoids all language barriers and speaks to all people. Not surprisingly, Jesus was a storyteller par excellence, and the bulk of his teaching is in story form. Like Father, like Son.

Story is the universal tongue. Everybody loves a story. All of us seem to be descended from that fabled king in *The Thousand and One Nights* who, night after night, begged Scheherazade to finish the story she'd begun the evening before. We flock to the movies to let Hollywood tell us a story. In fact, the whole multibillion-dollar film industry is built on our innate hunger for stories. Haven't we all pouted and pleaded for someone—parent, older sibling, or baby-sitter—to read us a story? We line our bookshelves with paperback thrillers and romances, and we follow our television favorites faithfully week after week. Some of us may prefer history over fiction, truth over fantasy, and some of us are more demanding than others about the quality and content of the stories we read, but the fact remains that we all love a story.

Even when we sleep, something in the subconscious takes fragments of the day's experiences and, in phantasmagoric forms, weaves them together with our hopes and fears, creating those stories we call dreams. I have been told that in some experiments in sensory deprivation where volunteers float in body-temperature water in darkened cubicles where they can see and hear nothing, the brain sometimes does the same thing, compensating for the lack of sensory input by making up its own stories. We're hard-wired for stories.

As a result, the storytellers have long been among the most important and influential people in any society. In preliterate cultures, the storyteller, usually one of the shamans, was the repository of the tribe's corporate memory, and hence the person who was most able to define the tribe's identity. He or she was the person who remembered the history of the tribe, the stories of its fortunes and adventures, its heroines and heroes, and recited them to the young as part of their coming-of-age ceremonies, and to the old when their sense of identity began to wane.

We may not have our shamans any longer, but we do have our Spielbergs and Lucases, our cinema celebrities and our popular novelists who are more than amply compensated for trying to satisfy our apparently insatiable appetite for stories. Stories not only entertain us, they have the power, for good or for ill, to shape our universe, to teach us our values, to tell us who we are, and to enable us to dream about who we might become. If real-life heroes or heroines aren't close at hand, fictional ones will serve to enable us to find meaning in our past and to fantasize about our future exploits.

For this reason, our choice of stories is important. Some stories ennoble us, some debase and corrupt us, while others simply entertain and distract us. William Bennett had a passion for increasing the moral literacy and strengthening the character of America's young people. Rather than write a manual of instructions, he compiled *The Book of Virtues,* a collection of stories that illustrate and encourage the growth of those virtues that build true moral character. As Bennett says, "In teaching these stories we engage in an act of renewal. We welcome our children to a common world, a world of shared ideals, to a community of moral persons."[2] Such is the power of story.

And what of the power of the biblical story, the one that gives us insight into our identity and an understanding of our place in the universe, the meaning of our existence? What story could be more important than this one? How do we tell it, and who will listen when we do?

The Spoken Word

The keyword is "listen." If the language of God is story, it's a story to be told and not simply one to be read. As Paul said, "Faith comes from what is heard, and what is heard comes through the word of Christ" (Romans

10:17). Long before any of the biblical books had been reduced to writing, they were spoken aloud; they were stories told from generation to generation. They came into being as what we call the oral tradition. They were spoken stories whose tellers employed, as one Jewish theologian put it, "artistic freedom as a method of teaching in order to make those distant faith experiences of the ancestors not only actual but present in a tangible way and to make it possible for the community to experience, at least partially, the enthusiasm and emotion of the biblical heroes."[3] It might be said that when the stories were finally written down, they were written not so much to be read as to be read *aloud.*

In other words, when the original tellers of the biblical story used their creative imaginations in telling it, they did so not to change the meaning of the story, but to do just the opposite, to preserve the text and to release the story into the imagination of their hearers. The New Testament word for this kind of storytelling is *anamnesis,* the word used by Jesus at the Last Supper, the word for *remembrance.* Literally, it means "to remember again" or "to unforget." Re-membering in this way becomes the opposite of dis-membering. In other words, it means to remember in such a way that the thing remembered comes alive in the present with all the power of the original event. The cure for our biblical amnesia is *anamnesis.*

For centuries before the invention of the printing press and the universal availability of books, the Christian church relied on good storytelling to get its message across. In a sense, Christians anticipated the concept of multimedia presentations. They were in the vanguard of those using the arts to communicate. Drama, the medieval mystery plays, the often fanciful stories from the lives of the saints, narrative hymns and chants, stained-glass windows illustrating some part of the biblical narrative, stations of the cross, and Christmas crèches were all used in an attempt to engage people through the power of story. With a few notable exceptions, we haven't done very well at imaginative storytelling in recent years.

Some have said that the pressure of the scientific establishment, argu-
ing as it does for what might be called propositional proof of all statements
about the truth, has caused the church to soft-pedal its narratives and to
rely more heavily on nouns rather than on verbs. They say we're more
likely, for example, to be content to say that God should be thought of as
a loving and generous parent than to go to the trouble of telling the story
of the prodigal son. The former may touch the mind or the heart, but the
latter will engage the imagination plus the mind and heart.

Some years ago a physician friend of mine in Denver so impressed the
other members of his group practice by his exemplary Christian life that
one of them finally asked him, "Will you explain the Christian faith to
me?" The doctor's reply was superb. "No," he said, "I won't. But I will tell
you the story of Jesus."

Preaching has suffered, too, through neglect of the art and neglect of
engaging the imagination. Many sermons are technically true, but they're
dull. There's an old joke about the difference between preachers and actors.
Actors, it is said, make fiction sound like fact, while preachers make fact
sound like fiction. That should be considered, if not a felony, at least a mis-
demeanor.

(Perhaps to balance it out, there's an equally old story about a gathering during which a famous actor was asked to recite the Twenty-third
Psalm. His performance was flawless and moving. At the end, someone
asked the local cleric to do the same thing. His recital was much less pro-
fessional and occasionally halting, but at the end the actor was in tears. "I
know the Psalm," he said, "but this man knows the Shepherd.")

The Word in Action

In the long run, the most effective way of telling the story is by making the
story visible. Jesus is, after all, the Word made flesh. John, who gave us that

description, seems to have had trouble distinguishing between the spoken and the visible word:

> We declare to you what was from the beginning, what we have heard, what we have seen with our eyes, what we have looked at and touched with our hands, concerning the word of life—this life was revealed, and we have seen it and testify to it, and declare to you the eternal life that was with the Father and was revealed to us—we declare to you what we have seen and heard so that you also may have fellowship with us; and truly our fellowship is with the Father and with his Son Jesus Christ. (1 John 1:1-3)

And in a similar vein James reminds the Christian community where they came from:

> In fulfillment of his own purpose he gave us birth by the word of truth, so that we would become a kind of first fruits of his creatures.... Therefore...welcome with meekness the implanted word that has the power to save your souls. But be doers of the word, and not merely hearers who deceive themselves. (James 1:18,21-22)

Any pastor will tell you that it's much easier to gather a crowd to *hear* the Word than it is to get a group interested in *doing* the Word. Bible studies abound, but biblical action groups—people involved in feeding the hungry, clothing the naked, housing the homeless, and defending the powerless—are a rarer breed.

If it does little else, the Creation lens that we've employed in rereading the story reveals the creative and active character of the Word. As we said earlier, it isn't merely a matter of *information;* it's also an *invitation* to participate in a community that is living the life described in the Scriptures. To put it another way, the Scriptures are the *script* for the drama performed by the community of faith. The apostles were able to proclaim the good news with great power because they stood in the midst of a community that resembled what they preached. The spoken word, in the mouth of one who lives the Word, is a convincing word.

A priest told me that he'd developed a new way of introducing newcomers and converts to the Christian faith. The old way, he said, was to enroll them in a lengthy educational program during which they would be taught all the essentials. He said that it was moderately successful, but that within a year or two a significant proportion of these converts had drifted away.

The new way, he said, was to challenge them to do two things: first, to worship with his congregation every Sunday for six months, and second, to volunteer a couple of hours a week in one of the church's outreach ministries such as a food bank, a homeless shelter, mentoring an at-risk child, or working on houses with Habitat for Humanity.

The combination was more effective than the classes, he said. Participation in the liturgy of Word and sacrament each week enabled the newcomers to learn, almost by osmosis, the values and principles of the Christian faith. And working in the outreach ministries confirmed that knowledge as they learned, by doing, just how those values and principles were to be put into action.

The Sword in Action

In Paul's famous description of "the whole armor of God," the Sword, "which is the word of God," is the only offensive weapon listed. All the others are for defense, but this sword is designed to slice through all untruths, to destroy the lies of the enemy, and to lay bare all of his stratagems. "Our struggle is not against enemies of blood and flesh, but against the rulers, against the authorities, against the cosmic powers of this present darkness, against the spiritual forces of evil in the heavenly places" (Ephesians 6:12). That's how Paul describes warfare in the new creation. The battle is spiritual. We don't go after those who oppose us with AK-47's, nor do we take out a contract on our enemies. Spiritual warfare calls for spiritual weapons.

The sword of violence, as we saw in an earlier chapter, failed to usher in the kingdom, and Jesus warns us that "all who take the sword will perish by the sword" (Matthew 26:52). Violence begets violence, and God's true shalom cannot be produced by something that is its polar opposite. The Sword of the Spirit, on the other hand, is a creative force that has the power to banish darkness and ignorance and to nourish the new community of faith inaugurated by the Resurrection.

A key difference between the old sword and the new is that the new one is not coercive. It reveals the truth and encourages us to receive it and walk in it, but it doesn't compel. We aren't driven into the kingdom. We're invited.

An old *Peanuts* cartoon pictures Lucy and Charlie Brown staring out a window at a ferocious rainstorm. Lucy voices her fear that the rain might continue until the whole world was flooded. Charlie Brown counters by quoting God's promise to Noah that never again would there be a flood "to destroy all flesh" (Genesis 9:15). Lucy replies that that makes her feel much better. And Charlie Brown turns to the audience and says, "Good theology has a way of doing that."

The devil's favorite tool in seeking the destruction of humankind is the half-truth, the sort of lie that sounds plausible because at least part of it

rings true. When Jesus did battle with the Tempter in the wilderness, his
only weapon was the Word of God. "It is written," he replied three times
and quoted the appropriate Scriptures to counter the devil's temptations.
Truth has the power to set us free. The Sword of the Spirit cuts straight
through the Tempter's deceptions.

Martin Luther was convinced of the power of the Word of God and
the truth of God to get the job done. In his famous hymn, "A Mighty
Fortress," he wrote,

And though this world with devils filled,
Should threaten to undo us,
We will not fear,
    for God hath willed
His truth to triumph through us.

A woman came to visit me when I was serving as bishop in Colorado.
My administrative assistant had sensed the lady's distress on the phone and
had recommended that I see her. When I asked her how I might help her,
she began to tell me a sad story about having been abandoned by her husband. "I've had to go back to work," she said, "but I don't seem to be able
to keep a job. Since I'm always the last hired, I'm the first fired. My teenage
son had to quit school to get a job just so we could eat." I thought she was
going to ask for financial assistance, but she continued, "Bishop, we're not
members of your church, but we go to our little church faithfully every
Sunday. I go to the Wednesday evening Bible study and the Friday night
prayer group, and we always tithe what little money we get. What am I
doing wrong?"

I said I didn't understand the question. She replied that her pastor had
told her that if she got her life right with the Lord, she wouldn't have any

more troubles, that Jesus would prosper everything that she did. "What am I doing wrong?" she repeated.

I'm afraid I laughed as I said, "You poor woman! You're the victim of clerical malpractice! Somebody has taken the devil's temptations to Jesus, gift-wrapped them, and handed them to you as though they were the gospel. Let me tell you what the *real* gospel says: Give yourself to God completely, do everything that God tells you to do, follow Jesus every day, play all your cards right, and with some luck you'll get crucified!"

Her expression suddenly changed, and she began to laugh too. "Oh, thank God," she said. "I can handle these little problems all right, but I couldn't handle them with a load of guilt, thinking that it was all my fault and that I was doing something wrong." And she left. A ten-minute conversation with the score: Sword of the Spirit—1, Devil—0.

C. S. Lewis said that he thought the devil worked not by putting things into our minds, but by keeping other things out. A friend who was working through a personal crisis in which his behavior had cost him his job and almost ruined his marriage told me that he couldn't sleep because he couldn't stop thinking about what he'd done. His torment was real and painful. I suspect that many of us have known that feeling at one time or another. "I'm guilty, I'm guilty," he kept saying.

"That's only half the truth," I said. "Just the part the devil wants you to hear. But he's hiding the best part. There is a bigger truth that he doesn't want you to remember. You are guilty, yes, but you are also forgiven. Both God and your wife have forgiven you. You have a completely fresh start, a brand-new beginning. Forgiveness is an act of new creation, and when you decide to receive that truth, you can leave the past behind." I wish I could say the transformation was immediate, but it wasn't. It took a little time, but when it came, it was complete. And another son of God entered into his rightful inheritance. Sword of the Spirit—2, Devil—still 0.

Paul advises us to *take* the Sword of the Spirit. Not to admire it, extol its virtues, or put it on display, but take it. A sword that remains in its sheath is nothing more than an ornament or an artifact. Something to be appraised on the *Antiques Roadshow*. But released from its scabbard and placed in the hands of a skillful warrior, it has great power.

I became [the church's] servant according to God's commission that was given to me for you, to make the word of God fully known, the mystery that has been hidden throughout the ages and generations but has now been revealed to his saints. To them God chose to make known how great among the Gentiles are the riches of the glory of this mystery, which is Christ in you, the hope of glory.

—COLOSSIANS 1:25-27

The only ultimate disaster, I have come to realize, is to feel ourselves to be at home here on earth. As long as we are aliens, we cannot forget our true homeland.

—MALCOLM MUGGERIDGE

To live in Jerusalem and not believe in miracles is not to be a realist.

—ANONYMOUS RABBI

EIGHT

THE MEANS OF GRACE
AND THE HOPE OF GLORY

New Creation Spirituality

A cartoon pictures a bearded, white-robed, sandal-shod prophet carrying a large placard through a crowded downtown street. The placard reads, "The end is not near—you'll have to learn to cope!"

Well, of course! And even if the end were expected tomorrow, we'd still have to learn to cope. The big question is how we do it. Whether we do it well or poorly depends in large measure on what resources we bring to the enterprise, and the nature of our spirituality determines just what those resources are.

It should be evident from the last three chapters that a spirituality of the new creation will be practiced in community with others. It will take the role of the Holy Spirit seriously, and it will be firmly rooted in Holy Scripture.

But it will also bring along some additional assumptions to undergird and inform its practice. The first is that the presence of God isn't determined by how we feel or even by our conscious awareness of that presence. The second is that God really wants us to succeed. A couple of stories may serve to illustrate what I mean.

When I was an undergraduate at the University of Colorado in 1951, I spent a couple of hours a week reading to a fellow student. His name was John, and he was blind.

One day I asked him how he lost his sight. He told me of an accident that happened when he was a teenager and how, at that point, he had simply given up on life. "When the accident happened and I knew that I would never see again, I felt that life had ended, as far as I was concerned. I was bitter and angry with God for letting it happen, and I took my anger out on everyone around me. I felt that since I had no future, I wouldn't lift a finger on my own behalf. Let others wait on me. I shut my bedroom door and refused to come out except for meals."

The man I knew was an eager learner and an earnest student, so I had to ask what had changed his attitude. He told me this story. "One day, in exasperation, my father came into my room and started giving me a lecture. He said he was tired of my feeling sorry for myself. He said that winter was coming, and it was my job to put up the storm windows. 'You get those windows up by suppertime tonight, or else!' he shouted, slamming the door on his way out.

"Well," said John, "that made me so angry that I resolved to do it! Muttering and cursing to myself, I groped my way out to the garage, found the windows, a stepladder, all the necessary tools, and I went to work. *They'll be sorry when I fall off the ladder and break my neck,* I thought, but little by little, groping my way around the house, I got the job done."

Then he stopped, and his sightless eyes misted up as he told me, "I later discovered that at no time during the day had my father ever been more than four or five feet from my side."

The first assumption is that God is present—no more than an arm's length away—whether we're aware of it or not.

Another story.

When I was eleven years old, one of the chores assigned to me by my father was to provide kindling wood for a small wood stove and the fireplace in our home in Thomasville, Georgia. I would scour the woods near our house, searching for the stumps of pine trees that had been cut down, stumps that I would pull out of the ground and hack into kindling with my Boy Scout hatchet. The good stumps were full of what we used to call "fat wood," wood so saturated with resin that it could be lit with a single match.

One day I found a large stump in an open field near the house and tried to unearth it. I literally pushed and pulled and crowbarred for hours, but the root system was so deep and large that I simply couldn't pull it out of the ground. I was still struggling when my father came home from his office, spotted me working, and came over to watch. "I think I see your problem," he said. "What's that?" I asked. "You're not using all your strength," he replied. I exploded and told him how hard I had worked and for how long. "No," he said, "you're not using all your strength." When I cooled down I asked him what he meant, and he said, "You haven't asked me to help you yet."

Second assumption: God is not only present—he's active and on our side. And the spirituality of the new creation is about using all your strength.

Vocabulary

It has become problematic to speak of spirituality these days. One complicating factor is that the very word *spiritual* has been devalued in our current conversation. For some people, it can mean "unreal." For example, some skeptical theologians speak of the resurrection of Jesus as a "spiritual truth," by which they mean that it didn't really happen as an event in time and space but was something that occurred only in the consciousness of Jesus' followers. It symbolizes the fact, they say, that the impression Jesus made on his disciples was so strong that he couldn't really die (that is, be forgotten) but has been raised (in a spiritual sense!) in the hearts and minds of those who believe in him.

Sometimes the word is used as a synonym for *noble* or *uplifting*. To think "spiritual" thoughts is to rise above the petty, mundane thinking that characterizes most of our daily lives—to think about beauty or music or poetry rather than bank balances and who's doing what to whom. Occasionally it means "impractical," or "otherworldly," as in, "He's too spiritual to notice that the garbage needs to be taken out." And in some circles it's equated with contacting or channeling the spirits of the dead, as in consulting a spiritualist.

All of these meanings confuse the issue. Jesus' resurrection body may have been a "spiritual body," in the sense that it was somehow different from the one he had before the Cross, but it was a real body, capable of eating and drinking, occupying space, and casting a shadow. And a truly spiritual person may indeed think noble and uplifting thoughts but will not draw a false division between the spiritual and the material. This person will probably be the first to notice that the garbage needs to be removed, and the only spirit she'll want to contact is the Holy Spirit.

Another complicating factor is that spirituality has become a growth industry, and like the designer deities described in the last chapter, there are almost as many varieties of it as there are practitioners. Thus, all sorts of people, from narcissistic celebrities to Mafia-type gangsters, can be heard to say, "I'm a very spiritual person." The problem with so many homegrown spiritualities is that they're the products of our own minds, and as such, they are incapable of leading us out of the shallows of our imaginations into the deeper "current of spirituality."

The spirituality of the new creation, however, springs not from the mind of the individual, but from a community that has a long history of both personal and corporate experience with the living God, a culture that has been passed down from one generation to another for thousands of years. This community has generated some recognizable family customs that have been developed and tested over the years, and thus, we can enter into a living tradition deeply rooted in foundational experience, even as it grows toward a promised future.

Christian spirituality is rooted in the person of the Holy Spirit through the community of the Spirit, the law of the Spirit, and the Book of the Spirit. And while there are several varieties of authentic Christian spirituality, they all involve certain practices and disciplines.

The finest guide I know to these basic characteristics of authentic Christian spirituality is Richard Foster's *Celebration of Discipline,* in which he describes the classic means of accessing the life of the Spirit. These disciplines, he says, "allow us to place ourselves before God so that he can transform us." And they're for everybody, not just the spiritually elite or those fortunate few who don't have to cope with jobs or family. They're for all disciples-in-training, or as this book might indicate, for all those who want to enter into the fullness of the new creation.

Evermore Dwelling in Him

The goal or purpose of all Christian spirituality is union with God, a state of being in which we literally share God's life and he shares ours. It's a mutual indwelling. It's the thing that Jesus described when he spoke of being the vine and his followers the branches: "Abide in me as I abide in you.... Apart from me you can do nothing" (John 15:4-5). And it's what he prayed for on the night before his crucifixion: "That they may all be one. As you, Father, are in me and I am in you, may they also be in us" (John 17:21). It's what the resurrected Christ did when he breathed the Holy Spirit into his followers. And it's what Paul refers to over thirty times when he speaks of being "in Christ." An ancient Communion prayer asks, "that we may evermore dwell in him, and he in us."

This mutual indwelling necessarily changes who and what we are and what we bring to any given situation. Paul's declaration to the Galatians, "It is no longer I who live, but it is Christ who lives in me" (2:20), ceases to sound like pious exaggeration and becomes a simple statement of fact. And it means that there can be no false dichotomy between our spirituality and our actions, between our piety and our practice. There is no antagonism between prayer and action. To pray without a willingness to act is slothful at best and blasphemous at worst. And to act without praying is presumptuous.

Brother Lawrence found that he could pick up a straw from the kitchen floor to the glory of God, and our spirituality embraces both the way we pray and the way we behave in the mall. We're invited to become what we are and what we were meant to be—part of the family, God's own beloved children.

A Two-Way Bridge

Our spirituality, moreover, is the vital link between what is and what will be, between our temporal reality and God's eternal reality, between our life now and the life of the age to come. The spirituality of the new creation will be seen as a bridge between the two, with traffic moving in both directions. It's a spirituality that enables us to *remember* the future. Our present experience will be modified by our anticipation of the promised things to come, and some of these promised things to come will sneak back from the future to infiltrate and enhance our present experience.

An ancient prayer, dating from the fifth century, seems to have this in mind when it says:

> O God of unchangeable power and eternal light: Look favorably on your whole Church, that wonderful and sacred mystery; by the effectual working of your providence, carry out in tranquillity the plan of salvation; let the whole world see and know that things which were cast down are being raised up, and things which had grown old are being made new, and that all things are being brought to their perfection by him through whom all things were made, your Son Jesus Christ our Lord; who lives and reigns with you, in the unity of the Holy Spirit, one God, for ever and ever. Amen.[1]

I love audacious prayer! This one is full of chutzpa—boldness and bravado—a kind of countercultural confidence in the fact that, despite all appearances, God is actually moving the whole created order forward to a glorious climax in which all will be made new. It has an element that seems to contradict the evidence of our senses. We see the things that grow old simply grow older until they die and decay, and the amount of entropy in the universe is increased. That's the effect of the second law of thermodynamics.

In our everyday experience, things move toward *dis*integration and not integration. (Except in the old Aggie joke about the tornado that hit the A&M campus and did eight million dollars' worth of improvement.) But that same law of thermodynamics allows for an exception. Things move toward disintegration *except in those cases in which fresh energy is added to the system*. The new creation is precisely that fresh energy. Our "outer nature" may indeed be wasting away as Paul put it, but inwardly we *are* being renewed day by day. The future is breaking into the present to give us a preview of coming attractions and to expedite the recovery of hope.

For me, one of the most productive images of this interaction is Eucharistic. By using our creative imagination, we can envision the altar of our church building as the near end of a much larger table that extends out through the back wall of the church and on into eternity. At the far end we can picture Jesus standing, presiding over the Messianic banquet, the marriage supper of the Lamb (Revelation 19:9). And seated all around the table at that far end, we can imagine those faithful who have gone before us into the heavenly realm. As we receive the sacrament, we can picture our hands reaching through the veil that separates time and eternity, reaching into the future to receive nourishment from that banquet and bringing it back into our present. It becomes a foretaste of good things yet to come, the down payment of a promised future. One of our modern liturgies calls for the person administering the sacrament to say, "The body of Christ, the bread of *heaven.*"

The Same New Thing

The practice of a spirituality of the new creation will not be very different from any of the other classic Christian paths. It will still include prayer, fasting, meditation, service to others, praise, joyous celebration, and the rest of the disciplines. What identifies it as different is more a matter of attitude and direction. It will bring to the traditional disciplines a particular state of mind and a set of assumptions drawn from viewing the biblical story through the Creation lens.

God is present and active. Therefore, God will always be seen as the primary actor in our lives. Depending on your point of view, the Bible can be read as the history of a people who had an encounter with God, or it can be read as the history of the God who created the universe and of the ways in which this God goes about revealing his presence and purposes in the world. New-creation spirituality isn't a matter of our search for God, but rather, God's search for us, and our willingness to be found by him. We are the ones Jesus had in mind when he said that he came to seek and to save the lost. It's about our willingness to surrender to the "Hound of Heaven" who pursues us "down the nights and down the days…down the arches of the years…down the labyrinthine ways."2 A woman once told me how her whole understanding of the Christian faith was transformed when she discovered that God was actually seeking her and not deliberately hiding from her.

New creation, like creation itself, is an exercise of divine power. Whatever the subject, new creation will preface all consideration with the words, "In the beginning God." If we speak of prayer, the Bible, worship, the sacraments, works of mercy or generosity, let it be known that God is the initiator of all. "We love because he first loved us" (1 John 4:19).

But new creation, as we've seen in earlier chapters, necessarily requires our active response and collaboration. If I can use a sports analogy, Jesus is like a player-coach who invites others to the big game, not by handing out tickets, but uniforms. On a practical level, this means that our spirituality is a joint effort. We had nothing to do with our conception and birth, but our rebirth is a different matter.

As Children

When you place the Creation filter over the biblical story, the image of new birth takes center stage. What Jesus said to Nicodemus one way—you must be born again—he said to many others in a different fashion. Unless we become like children, he said, we can never enter the kingdom.

That's a pretty tall order for many of us. We find it hard to abandon our need to be thought of as grown up and mature! A second-century theologian speculated that Adam and Eve were created as young children, and that their sin involved trying to grow up too fast, ignoring the fact that maturity takes time. (My wife reminds me that it's *always* too soon to try to be autonomous!) C. S. Lewis said: "When I was ten I read fairy tales in secret and would have been ashamed if I had been found doing so. Now that I am fifty I read them openly. When I became a man I put away childish things, including the fear of childishness and the desire to be very grown up."[3]

One of the wonderful things about children is that they can still be surprised. And surprise seems to be one of the doors that leads into the kingdom. Praise, for example, begins as a spontaneous gasp of wonder at the overwhelming goodness of God and God's *amazing* grace. If you've ever played peekaboo with a small child, you know the capacity for joy that surprise can have. Each time you pop out of hiding, it seems to the child to be a new and fresh experience, and the sense of delight becomes more intense each time you do it. One of the saddest aspects of our culture is our inability—or our unwillingness—to be surprised. "Blessed are those who expect nothing, for they shall not be disappointed" seems to be our generation's beatitude. Pity the poor folk who will never permit themselves to be surprised, who always respond to everything with, "Been there! Done that!" What a dull existence!

Jesus invites us to look at everything that surrounds us with a sense of anticipation that God will pop out of hiding any minute now and overwhelm us with his joy, and with a childlike heart that never needs to adopt a jaded and world-weary pose. A truly mature spirituality will never abandon its childlike delight in the goodness of God. A sixth-century desert monk, known for his wise spiritual direction, said, "I am a fool, and I cannot bear to keep secret how wonderful God is!"

New creation is like the new wine that Jesus speaks of. It needs room to develop, a space to grow in. It needs the flexible nature of a true child-like spirit in which to ferment. As Jesus says, new wine needs fresh wine-skins. The expansion will burst the brittle leather of the old ones. "I thank you, Father, Lord of heaven and earth, because you have hidden these things from the wise and the intelligent and have revealed them to infants," he said (Matthew 11:25).

We're all apprentices in love, and one of the most attractive aspects of our pilgrimage is that it seems to have no end. There's always room to grow. Can finite creatures ever exhaust the joy of constant learning and progress in our knowledge of the height, the depth, the length, and the breadth of God's love? God's mercies are new every morning, and so may our response to them be. New creation means that every day opens with a fresh potential for growth and development, and that in turn brings the promise that life in Christ need never grow dull and boring. My not-so-secret desire is that when I die, at seventy-five, eighty-five, or ninety-five, the preacher at my funeral may be able to say, "What a shame! Cut down in his prime!"

Restless and Dissatisfied

Ironically, this very awareness of growth brings with it a certain sense of restlessness and dissatisfaction. Those may sound like strange words to use in describing our spirituality, but both seem to be necessary to a creative encounter with the living and very active God.

Our restlessness is the kind described by Augustine: "Our souls are restless until they rest in thee." To become "prisoners of hope" means to catch a vision of God's promised future and to find it difficult to rest until we see more signs of its fulfillment. We become dissatisfied with things as they are because we've caught a vision of what they might be. A holy restlessness is what saves our spirituality from becoming too "spiritual" in the superficial sense.

But this restlessness will be a *blessed* restlessness of the sort described in several of the Beatitudes. There's the restlessness of those who mourn, of those who hunger and thirst, and of those who make peace.

We mourn over the broken state of our own souls and that of the society around us, but we do so in the light of the promise that we shall be comforted.

We hunger and thirst for righteousness because we know that righteousness is part of what God has promised. And we know that one of the Bible's main themes is, as Elie Wiesel puts it, the "centrality of justice."

Mourning and hungering and knowing that we aren't called to be mere spectators, but fellow workers together with God, we'll be peacemakers. Peace is a precious commodity, and there isn't enough of it to go around. Besides, that's what children of God do. God is the author of shalom, and God's children will bear the family resemblance.

But we'll be careful to be peacemakers and not peacekeepers. Peace-*keepers* are likely to overlook the causes of pain and suffering, to avoid dealing with it in order to maintain some kind of equilibrium regardless of what it may be based on. Peacekeepers prefer the status quo and are apt to tell the hungry to quiet down lest they disturb the sleep of the overfed.

In God's typically paradoxical fashion, our restlessness will be complemented by a rest*ful*ness, also typified by several of the Beatitudes. It will be restful because it is so conscious of the creative activity of God. As the author of the epistle to the Hebrews put it, "A sabbath rest still remains for the people of God" (Hebrews 4:9).

We'll be merciful because we've already begun to receive mercy.

We'll be poor in spirit, knowing our need for God's strength, and in our spiritual poverty we will experience God's power, the kingdom of heaven.

We'll be pure in heart because our hearts of stone have begun to be replaced by the heart of flesh, and seeing this, we will see God.

We'll be meek—gentle in spirit—because our trust is not in our own strength, the "devices and desires of our own hearts," but in the mercy and power of the God who is making all things new.

The Courage to Hope

The new creation comes alive in us when we begin to notice little fragments of hope washing up on the sands of our consciousness. It begins when our dissatisfaction with what *is* leads us to hope for what *might be*. And it blossoms into life when we start to dream God's dream of true shalom and, through a process that defies complete explanation, find the courage to call that dream reality rather than illusion.

There's an enemy of hope abroad in our culture trying to convince us that only the present counts, that neither the past nor the future have any reality. The past is gone, it says, and the future hasn't happened yet. But this viewpoint is hopelessly earthbound. "The past exists in God's remembering it, and the future in his anticipating it; and what is remembered and anticipated in the life of God is not reduced to a present moment but rather spans and enables all moments," says a modern theologian.[4]

There's a sense in which the present moment is all we have to work with. The past is past and the future has not yet arrived. But that's only part of the truth. What is past has shaped us for the present moment, and therefore, we are carriers of it—we embody, to some degree, all that has gone before. And what we believe about the future determines, in large measure, how we use the present moment. And whether we use all our strength.

As we've seen over and over again, new-creation spirituality will be strongly biblical. That may sound like a threat to some who haven't yet taken the time to study the Book.

If you're one of those people for whom the Bible is still largely a mystery, my advice is, "Don't despair." You can remedy the lack by investing as little as fifteen minutes a day over the space of a year. The *One-Year Bible,* available in a variety of translations, is all you need. Don't worry about the parts that seem difficult or incomprehensible, and don't worry overmuch about *interpreting* the Bible until you've *read* the Bible. We need to know what it says before we get bogged down in what it means.

Unfortunately, in our culture, *biblical* has often been associated with either "dull" or "narrow-minded" and "judgmental." Nothing could be further from the truth. Being biblical simply means taking seriously the written record of how God used a particular group of people to reveal himself in human history. It's not always a pretty story, and parts of it are mystifying while others look pretty bloodthirsty. But it certainly isn't dull. And if you embrace the whole story, you'll find your mind being released from narrow judgments as it is stretched and expanded.

Being biblical means looking at Jesus as a real person rather than as a stained-glass image, a person who worked and sweated and talked until he was blue in the face to a strange group of followers, attempting to get them to share his vision of the Father so that they might carry on what he had begun. In the process, he managed to alienate a large number of his compatriots, enrage both the civil and religious authorities, and finally get himself executed as a common criminal.

Being biblical means entering the exciting and mysterious realm of creation and new creation, the realm of resurrection where all things can be made new because of the unfathomable depths of the heart of the loving God who dreams of a better world and enters into it to make the dream come true.

Being biblical means to enter into dialogue with all of human experience with a mixture of confidence, expectancy, and humility. The biblical person will not pretend to know more than has been revealed, but neither will he or she conceal what has been made clear. We come, neither as masters of all the secrets of the universe nor as blind gropers after some shred of truth and enlightenment, but rather as awestruck apprentices who have been given enough light to continue the journey with confidence and conviction.

But what's the goal of the journey?

The Glory to Be Revealed

In an unforgettable scene in the movie *Field of Dreams,* the protagonist, played by Kevin Costner, converses with a long-dead baseball player who has mysteriously appeared on the baseball diamond Costner has constructed. ("If you build it, they will come.") The ballplayer looks around wonderingly and asks, "Is this heaven?" Costner laughs and replies, "No, it's Iowa." The other says, "I could have sworn it was heaven." His curiosity engaged, Costner asks, "*Is* there a heaven?" To which the ballplayer says, "Oh yeah! It's where dreams come true." Costner then glances behind him to his house and sees an idyllic scene. It is twilight on a warm summer evening. His wife and young daughter are sitting in the porch swing, laughing, enjoying each other's company, and perhaps sharing a pitcher of iced tea. He reflects for a moment, then says, "Maybe this *is* heaven."

It's a pretty scene and seems to say something profound, maybe something about being thankful for the good times. But on a deeper level, it's deceptive. We know, don't we, that it isn't heaven. We know that it's all temporary. Summer won't last forever, and eventually his wife and daughter and he himself are going to grow old and die. Our dreams and our hopes for the future will inevitably disappoint us if they're grounded only in this life.

In one of the most profound one-sentence definitions of human existence, Augustine wrote in his *Confessions,* "Thou hast made us for thyself, O God, and our souls are restless till they rest in thee." Regardless of how hard we try, the "God-shaped hole" inside each of us cannot be filled by anything but God. All of our earthly hopes end in death and decay. You and I are not made for time alone, but for eternity. Iowa is not enough. In the final analysis, all our hopes must end in heaven or they end in frustration. There's nothing earthly we can hope for that will not ultimately disappoint us and leave us asking for something more. "Is that all there is?" is more than the title of a song.

Shortly before he died in 1990, the novelist Walker Percy, was quoted as saying, "This life is much too much trouble, far too strange, to arrive at the end of it and then be asked what you make of it, and then have to answer, 'Scientific humanism.' " Then, with an almost playful audacity, he added, "That won't do. A poor show. Life is a mystery, love is a delight. Therefore I take it as axiomatic that one should settle for nothing less than the infinite mystery and the infinite delight, i.e., God. In fact, I demand it. I refuse to settle for anything less!"[5]

The deepest longing of the human heart, the one thing we groan for inwardly, stems from the fact that though we've been cast out of Eden, the memory of Eden hasn't been cast out of us. We long for wholeness, for the restoration of the image and likeness of God in our souls.

C. S. Lewis said, "The sweetest thing in my life has been the longing to find the place where all the beauty came from." In one sense at least the beauty comes from the future, from that "hope of glory" to which Paul refers. Though we can't get back to the original Eden, we can—and are destined to—move forward into the new heaven and the new earth spoken of by the prophets. Though we normally identify ourselves by what we've been in the past and what we are at the present, our identity isn't fully defined until we add what we shall be. "Beloved, we are God's children *now;* what we will be has not yet been revealed. What we do know is this: when he is revealed, we will be like him" (1 John 3:2).

The biblical story describes us as caught up in time, but only as "aliens and exiles" (1 Peter 2:11). Somehow we live in one place but belong to another. As Paul described it, "Our citizenship is in heaven, and…[Jesus] will transform the body of our humiliation that it may be conformed to the body of his glory" (Philippians 3:20-21). In another context he tells us that he is convinced that "the sufferings of this present time are not worth comparing with the glory about to be revealed to us" (Romans 8:18). Our earthly sojourn is important, as is the way we conduct ourselves in it. But it's temporary. It's worth listening to Paul again as he describes the effect of this overlapping of time and eternity. The words are from his second letter to the church at Corinth and are taken from chapters 3, 4, and 5. While these chapters contain much more material, I have attempted simply to follow one thread of what he says:

> Since, then, we have such a hope, we act with great boldness.…
> Now the Lord is the Spirit, and where the Spirit of the Lord is,
> there is freedom. And all of us, with unveiled faces, seeing the glory
> of the Lord as though reflected in a mirror, are being transformed
> into the same image from one degree of glory to another.… So we
> do not lose heart. Even though our outer nature is wasting away,
> our inner nature is being renewed day by day. For this slight
> momentary affliction [Paul's definition of life on earth] is preparing
> for us an eternal weight of glory beyond all measure.… For we
> know that if the earthly tent we live in is destroyed, we have a

building from God, a house not made with hands, eternal in the heavens. (3:12,17-18; 4:16-17; 5:1)

The Creation lens takes us back to the beginning of the story, to Adam and Eve. And it helps us remember what God said to them about the tree of the knowledge of good and evil—"in the day that you eat of it you shall die" (Genesis 2:17). Apparently, death wasn't part of the original design. Planned obsolescence wasn't on God's mind. We were made for eternity. And we can't read the biblical story without seeing just how determined God is to see that his original vision is eventually brought to reality. The new creation isn't complete until it includes the new heaven and the new earth.

In my own branch of the Christian church, we have, unfortunately, heard little teaching on heaven in recent years. My guess is that we've listened too much to the critics who say that to talk of heaven overmuch is a form of escapism that could tempt us to ignore the very real problems of the present time. We've mistakenly assumed that "relevance," which is a virtue greatly to be desired, must limit itself to the *immediate* needs of people.

As a result we've soft-pedaled the *ultimate* needs of people. Yes, the church must be vigorously concerned about what the Bible calls justice and shalom. The evidence is unmistakable. God is interested in these things. God has concern for the "widows and orphans"—the helpless, the outcasts, the oppressed—and a Christian community that doesn't concern itself with such matters is probably just playing church.

But one day we'll die, and the problems of "hunger, fear, injustice, and oppression" will on that day end for each of us. The question of what comes next is not irrelevant at all. The philosopher Peter Kreeft observes, "If life on earth is not a road to heaven, then it is a treadmill, a merry-go-round minus the merry."

We've never lacked those critics who remind us that heaven has often been the tool of oppressors. Tyrants, from slave owners to modern-day autocrats, have used it to divert the attention of their victims from their misery and exploitation, telling them to ignore their immediate poverty and concentrate on their heavenly reward. However true that may be, it's hardly a reason for downplaying one of the great themes of Jesus' teaching. He says: "Lay up for yourselves treasures in heaven," "I go to prepare a place for you," "In my Father's house there are many mansions," "Today you will be with me in paradise." And as Paul said, "If for this life only we have hoped in Christ, we are of all people most to be pitied."

Far from being a form of escapism, the promise of heaven is what keeps us from being unrealistic, from trying to fill a heavenly void with earthly materials. And paradoxically, contemplation of heaven does have an earthly benefit. The more we learn about the future glory, the more likely we'll be to try to turn our present realities into replicas, admittedly limited, of that glory. When we look at the character of heaven, there's a good chance that we'll want to borrow the pattern and use it for our own life in the here and now. We'll want to decorate our houses with what one writer calls "the furniture of heaven." When we consider that many of the people we now know are likely to be our companions in eternity, we discover that it's in our interest to pay more attention to those relationships now.

There's another reason for reminding ourselves of the hope of heaven. There's something else going on in our society, indeed, all over the world, that should bring the heavenly promises front and center again. One of the tragic legacies of the AIDS epidemic is that we have a larger number of younger people facing death than at any time since the great influenza epidemic of the early part of the last century. We all know that old people die, but today there are many in their twenties, thirties, and forties facing the same fate. It would be cruel and unusual punishment to withhold such a glorious biblical promise from those who anticipate what can only be called an untimely end.

And what can we say to those people in various parts of the world for whom, realistically speaking, there is no relief in the foreseeable future from their miserable living conditions? Does the gospel have nothing to say to them? Of course it does! The hope of glory has the same power today as it did in the waning days of the Roman Empire, when a series of persecutions threatened the church's very existence. It still has the ability to breathe new life into the hearts of hounded minorities and to give them a dignity heretofore denied them.

At the Lambeth Conference in 1978, a Sudanese bishop told a remarkable story. Christians in the southern Sudan were being persecuted by the Muslim majority in the north, just as they still are at the time of this writing. They were being hounded from town to town and often were forced to take refuge in the bush. They had no certain dwelling place, and their suffering was great. Nonetheless, said the bishop, God had been very good to them. He'd given them new music, new songs and hymns with which to praise him. "Since we didn't have access to printing presses, we wrote the words and music down in school children's copy books and passed them around." A people who praise may suffer greatly, but they cannot be defeated.

The bishop's words immediately brought to mind Paul's description of his first-century Christians who suffered "afflictions, hardships, calamities, beatings, imprisonments, riots, labors, sleepless nights, hunger.... [Who were] treated as imposters, and yet are true; as unknown, and yet are well known; as dying, and see—we are alive; as punished, and yet not killed; as sorrowful, yet always rejoicing; as poor, yet making many rich; as having nothing, and yet possessing everything" (2 Corinthians 6:4-5,8-10). Is the hope of heaven still relevant? You betcha!

Admittedly, the biblical pictures of heaven and eternity are framed by symbol and metaphor. The details of heavenly life are more general than specific. We do know that the life of the age to come (a literal interpretation of the phrase usually translated "eternal life") will be marked by freedom from all earthly bondage, by joy and praise, by the healing of all wounds, by seeing God face to face, and by the wiping away of tears. (I hope an exception will be made for tears of joy.) But architectural details of the "many mansions" (wayside inns) are lacking. There's no word about the menu at the supper of the Lamb, nothing about the style of the white robes, or the details of daily life. (Is it even appropriate to speak of daily life in eternity?) It's probably useless to try to decipher the symbols and metaphors, to read more into them than has actually been revealed. Besides, our imaginations are so *limited!* I think it's far better to wait for that glorious moment when we experience what they symbolize, and in our awestruck wonder, say to ourselves—between the alleluias—"Aha! So *that's* what it meant!"

For me, one of the most poignant descriptions of this reality comes from C. S. Lewis's children's book *The Last Battle,* the final volume of the Narnia series. Aslan, the great Lion and Christ figure, is speaking to the children whose adventures in Narnia are the subject of the series. "All of you are—as you used to call it in the Shadow-Lands—dead. The term is over: the holidays have begun. The dream is ended: this is the morning." Lewis continues, "The things that began to happen after that were so great and beautiful that I cannot write them. And for us this is the end of all the stories, and we can most truly say that all lived happily ever after. But for them it was only the beginning of the real story. All their life in this world and all their adventures in Narnia had only been the cover and the title page; now at last they were beginning Chapter One of the Great Story…which goes on forever; in which every chapter is better than the one before."[6]

Such must have been the conviction that led Dag Hammarskjöld to write, "For all that has been—Thanks! For all that shall be—Yes!"

Hope is the ability to hear the melody of the future, and faith is the courage to dance to it today.

ROMANCING THE WORD

One of my closest friends from high-school days is Jewish and came from the sort of family that is usually described as nonobservant. When he was in his midfifties, the son of one of his neighbors was having his Bar Mitzvah, and my friend decided to attend. It was the first time he had witnessed the ceremony, and as he watched the cantor walk down the aisle with the Torah scroll, he told me that he was suddenly gripped by an overwhelming urge that seemed to come from somewhere deep within his psyche. To his own surprise he got up from his pew, walked into the aisle, and kissed the scroll. That act was the beginning of a journey that led him to have his own Bar Mitzvah at the age of fifty-eight. Liturgy can be a powerful thing.

My friend's story reminded me of a haunting scene in one of Chaim Potok's novels in which, on the feast of *Simcha Torah* (the giving of the Law), a young rabbi, holding the Torah to his breast and dancing, overwhelmed by the privilege of bearing the sacred Word, has a strange thought: *I wonder if my Christian friends ever dance with their Bibles?*

In my own tradition the closest we ever come to such a thing is a gospel procession in which a deacon carries the gospel Book down the center aisle to the middle of the church and reads from it. True, it can be impressive, but you'll rarely catch a deacon dancing.

In a sense, the traditional eucharistic liturgy itself might be described as the Christian's tribal dance. It has most of the major elements, including color and special costumes, and it involves at least some form of movement to music. The officiants and the choir usually march in and out to hymns; there is a rhythm of sitting, standing, and kneeling; in some cases, people make gestures such as the sign of the cross, and worshipers at one point get up and leave their pews to go to receive Communion. It is a kind of dance, although admittedly a very slow and solemn one.

Who would have thought up such a thing as dancing with the Word? It must have come from a heart like that of the psalmist who proclaimed, "Your word is a lamp to my feet and a light to my path…. Oh, how I love your law! It is my meditation all day long…. Sing to the LORD a new song, his praise in the assembly of the faithful…. Let them praise his name with dancing, making melody to him with tambourine and lyre" (Psalm 119:105,97; 149:1,3). Wherever it comes from, it is a remarkable way of acting out a sense of praise and wonder by those who know the limits of their own understanding and are actively seeking a wisdom from above that transcends their own experience. Dancing with the Bible is a form of recognizing its intrinsic power and paying homage to it.

Quite apart from the many hair-splitting squabbles about the Bible's authority and inspiration—those arguments that often send otherwise sensible Christians running to the barricades—the Book does have an undeniable power. For thousands of years people from hundreds of ethnic and cultural backgrounds and in a multitude of historical and social settings have been fed, nourished, and, indeed, challenged by the Scriptures. The story is told of Henry VIII's personal physician, who was given an English translation of the four Gospels. After reading them he declared, "Either these are not the true Gospels, or we are not Christians!"

Dance was an integral part of ancient worship, so common that it didn't require much special mention in the Bible. It was part and parcel of worshipful celebrations. "Singers and dancers alike say, 'All my springs are in you'" (Psalm 87:7).

The fairly recent excavations of the southern steps leading up to the Temple Mount in Jerusalem reveal a rhythmic pattern in their design—two short steps to one long one—as though they had been carved not just for climbing, but for dancing. When this was first pointed out to me by an Israeli archaeologist, what popped into my mind was a picture of Tevye from *Fiddler on the Roof,* dancing and singing about his longing to be a rich man so that he could spend all day with the Holy Book.

What you have just read, if you've made it this far, is the result of many years of my own dancing with the Bible, of my own romancing the Word. I don't think I would have used such phrases except for the fact that I once heard of a French theologian who was said to have had "an almost erotic relationship with the New Testament." Ah, the French! My background is more Germanic and Italian, but you get the idea.

Like everyone else who reads it, I find many parts of the Bible troubling and confusing, but at the same time, I have discovered that the more I squeeze it, the more juice comes out. An eloquent preacher, Barbara Brown Taylor, counsels clergy to "preach the terrors," that is, to wrestle with the problematic passages—as Jacob wrestled with the Lord—until they give you a blessing.

I hope I've encouraged you to dance with your Bible and to find some fresh blessings. "Where words come to an end, the dance begins."

QUESTIONS FOR STUDY
AND DISCUSSION

Introduction

- When you think of heaven, what images come to mind?
- Peter says we should always be ready to give a reason for the hope that is in us. (1 Peter 3:15) What reason would you give?
- Who are the hopeful people you know or have heard of—those who triumph over the circumstances of their lives? What makes this hope and triumph possible?
- Do you ever find yourself in the situation described in this chapter under the heading *The Erosion of Hope*? If so, how do you generally respond?
- What are the effects of memory loss? What are the effects of the loss of biblical memory?
- Through what lens do you read the Bible?

Chapter 1

- What kind of outline helps you keep the biblical story clear?

- "Only when we understand what was lost will we be able to appreciate how it might be recovered." We've all lost things we value. How do we generally compensate for what is lost or recover from the loss?
- "Life has both purpose and direction." What are the things that obscure life's purpose and direction in your personal life? in your family life? in your church life?
- When confronted with evil—close at hand or in other parts of the world—what is it that makes us feel that "it's not supposed to be that way?"
- Adam and Eve tried to hide from God (Genesis 3:8). How do we do the same thing?
- What examples can you give of God's judgment being an act of mercy?

Chapter 2

- Do you begrudge God the right to define what is good—for you and for those you love? If so, how does this feeling manifest itself in your actions or attitudes?
- Keeping in mind the images of the Ark, the Law, and the Sword, what is your preferred method of dealing with problems?
- Give examples of how each of those three approaches—Ark, Law, and Sword—are used in responding to problems.
- Recall G. K. Chesterton's remark about the ways of God having been "found difficult and not tried." Was that a cheap shot? In what ways might people actually try, yet still find God's ways too hard?
- Why do people sometimes find God's ways so difficult?

Chapter 3

- What are God's promises for? What is their purpose?
- In 2 Corinthians 1:20 we read that in Christ "every one of God's promises is a 'Yes.'" What promises of God are central in your life and experience?
- Peter writes that through God's "precious and very great promises" we're enabled to "escape from the corruption that is in the world because of lust, and may become participants of the divine nature" (2 Peter 1:4). In your own words, how would you explain the effect of living by God's promises?
- How does the Creation lens help you understand the story of Jesus?
- What does the image of being "born again" mean to you? Can you be "born again" again?

Chapter 4

- Do you regard the Resurrection as metaphorical or historical? What difference does your view of the Resurrection make in your life? in the life of your family? in the life of your church?
- How has your image of God developed or changed over the years?
- What events in your life have exposed your spiritual poverty?
- What would a "revolution of rising expectations" look like in your life?

Chapter 5

- Where do you find community?
- What is your primary community?

- What would the church need to look like in order to become a primary community? (See Acts 2:42.)
- What is the difference between entertaining guests and offering hospitality?
- When you think of baptism and leaving the "old life" behind, what "old clothes" still beckon to you? (See Ephesians 4:22-24; Colossians 3:12-17.)

Chapter 6

- Have you ever had the sort of soul-searching experience described in this chapter's opening pages?
- What happens when we rely solely on our own natural abilities?
- Can you give examples of grace building on nature or even triumphing over it?
- How do you deal personally with the tension between law and grace?
- In what instances might you feel that forgiveness lets the wrong-doer off too easily?
- How has the Spirit's power been demonstrated in your life?

Chapter 7

- In what ways have you found the Bible to be a "subversive" book?
- What are some of the "designer gods" you've encountered in your own life? in the culture at large?
- What biblical stories have had the most impact on your life?
- What parts of the biblical story represent the script for the life of your church?

• Where would you start if you wanted to tell the biblical story to someone who had never heard it?

Chapter 8

• What are the major "means of grace" for you—the channels through which God strengthens and encourages you?
• What illustration from your own life can you think of to support the statement that God is present whether or not we're aware of his presence? (See 2 Kings 6:15-17; Psalm 139.)
• What does it mean to say that God is "active and on our side"?
• How can we help one another become more "childlike" (a quality Jesus commends in Matthew 18:3)?
• What longing does the phrase "the hope of glory" awaken in you? (See Colossians 1:27.)

NOTES

Introduction

1. Thomas Berry, *The New Story,* Teilhard Studies, no. 1 (Chambersburg, Pa.: Anima Books, 1978).

2. "Have you not read in the book of Moses...how God said to him, 'I am the God of Abraham, the God of Isaac, and the God of Jacob'? He is the God not of the dead, but of the living" (Mark 12:26-27).

3. Thomas Cahill, *The Gift of the Jews* (New York: Doubleday, 1998), 7.

4. Berry, *The New Story.*

Chapter 1

1. James Weldon Johnson, "The Creation," in *God's Trombones* (New York: The Viking Press, 1927, renewed 1955), 19-20.

2. *Book of Common Prayer* (New York: Church Hymnal Corporation, 1977), 392.

3. J. R. R. Tolkien, letter to Christopher Tolkien, 30 January 1945.

4. Frederick Buechner, *Peculiar Treasures* (New York: Harper & Row, 1979), 35.

5. William Willimon, *Journal for Preachers,* Easter 1999, quoted in Martin E. Marty, *Context* (15 August 1999).

Chapter 2

1. Richard B. Hays, *The Moral Vision of the New Testament* (San Francisco: HarperSanFrancisco, 1996), 202.
2. *Noye's Fludde,* medieval play, musical arrangement in 1958 by Benjamin Britten (1913–1976).
3. Ted Koppel, "The Last Word," commencement address at Duke University, Durham, North Carolina, 10 May 1987. Quoted in Robert H. Bork, *The Tempting of America: The Political Seduction of the Law* (New York: The Free Press, 1989), 164.
4. Cahill, *The Gifts of the Jews,* 142.
5. From a lecture given in Denver, 1988.
6. *Book of Common Prayer,* 370.
7. Cahill, *The Gifts of the Jews,* 53.
8. Carl Braaten in Pinchas Lapide, *The Resurrection of Jesus* (London: SPCK, 1984), 24.

Chapter 3

1. "It is more blessed to give than to receive" (Acts 20:35); the blessing of the bread and cup at the Last Supper (1 Corinthians 11:23-25).
2. Walter Russell Bowie, "Lord Christ, when first thou cam'st to earth." *The Hymnal 1982* (New York: Church Publishing, June 1979), 598.
3. Abraham Joshua Heschel, quoted in Jon Levenson, *The Sabbath: Its Meaning for Modern Man* (New York: Farrar, Straus, and Giroux, 1975).
4. Jim Wallis, *The Call to Conversion* (New York: Harper & Row, 1981), 6.
5. Gregory Dix, *The Shape of the Liturgy* (1945, reprint, New York: Seabury, 1982), 743f.

Chapter 4

1. John Updike, *Telephone Poles and Other Poems* (New York: Knopf, 1961).
2. C. S. Lewis, *Prince Caspian* (New York: MacMillan, 1986), chap. 10.
3. Macrina Wiederkehr, *Seasons of Your Heart: Prayers and Reflections* (San Francisco: HarperSanFrancisco, 1991), 97.

Chapter 5

1. Dietrich Bonhoeffer, *Life Together* (San Francisco: HarperSanFrancisco, 1954), 18.
2. *Book of Common Prayer,* 306.
3. St. Cyril from *Catechetical Lectures of St. Cyril,* 347-8.
4. *Book of Common Prayer,* 302.

Chapter 6

1. Thomas A. Smail, *The Forgotten Father* (London: Hodder and Stoughton, 1980).

Chapter 7

1. Helen Keller, *The Story of My Life* (New York: Doubleday, July 1991 reissue).
2. William J. Bennett, *The Book of Virtues* (New York: Simon & Schuster, 1993), 12.
3. Pinchas Lapide, *The Resurrection of Jesus* (London: SPCK, 1983), 101.

Chapter 8

1. *Book of Common Prayer,* 280.

2. Francis Thompson, "The Hound of Heaven," in *The Works of Francis Thompson,* 2 vols. (New York: Charles Scribner's Sons, 1913).

3. C. S. Lewis, "On Three Ways of Writing for Children," in *Of Other Worlds: Essays and Stories,* ed. Walter Hooper (New York: Harcourt, Brace, Jovanovich, 1975).

4. Robert W. Jenson, "The American People," *First Things* (April 1999).

5. Walker Percy, "Questions They Never Asked Me" in *Signposts in a Strange Land* (New York: Farrar, Straus, Giroux, 1991).

6. C. S. Lewis, *The Last Battle* (New York: MacMillan, 1956), 173.

ABOUT THE AUTHOR

WILLIAM C. FREY, a well-known leader in the renewal movement of the Episcopal church in the Anglican Communion, served as an ordained priest in parishes in Colorado and New Mexico from 1955 to 1962. He and his wife, Barbara, also served as missionaries in Costa Rica and Guatemala in the late sixties and early seventies. In Costa Rica, he served as rector of a parish, teacher in a small seminary, and translator and editor of Christian books. He was elected bishop of the Episcopal Church in Guatemala in 1967, where his peacemaking activities resulted in his expulsion from the country in 1971. He was elected bishop of the Episcopal Church in Colorado in 1972 and served in this role for eighteen years. He also served as dean of the Trinity Episcopal School for Ministry in Ambridge, Pennsylvania, from 1990 to 1996. Now retired, Bishop Frey and Barbara live in San Antonio, Texas. They continue to lead conferences and retreats around the world.